What if we actually lived out what we shouted about on Sunday mornings? What if we authentically applied what we read in the Bible? What if we consistently loved those who persecuted us and lied to us, and we embraced people who are just searching for God in all the wrong places? We would upset the world! In this book, my mentor, friend, and oversight pastor, Tim Ross, shares practical knowledge and wisdom that I have had the opportunity to experience personally. I believe these truths are the key to shifting our culture and re-presenting Christ to the world.

Michael Todd
Lead Pastor of Transformation Church

When did we become so accustomed to the world around us that we forgot to live by the world within us? The world that reflects the Creator we serve. The life that doesn't fit in but stands out. This book will inspire you to stop blending and start standing. Allow the Holy Spirit to transform you from the inside out, and soon you will find yourself turning the world upside down.

Charlotte Gambill
Bestselling author, speaker,
and lead pastor of LIFE Church

Tim Ross is one of the greatest communicators of Christian truth I have ever met. The thing I love most about him is that he is the same off the stage as he is on the stage. He lives the truth he teaches with integrity, humility, and passion. There is revelation in these pages, and I commend *Upset the World* to you with all my heart.

Mike Pilavachi
Founder of Soul Survivor Watford and Soul Survivor UK

Upset the World is not your ordinary evangelism manual. Tim Ross brings fresh revelation and much-needed encouragement to anyone in the body of Christ who wants to share their faith. Through sound biblical teaching, time-tested practical advice, and captivating personal stories, Tim takes the complexity out of witnessing and shows how anyone—yes, even you!—can upset the world for Jesus Christ.

Jimmy Evans
Bestselling author, speaker,
and Senior Pastor of Gateway Church

Reading my friend Tim Ross's new book, *Upset the World*, is like taking a deep breath of fresh air. His unique take on relational evangelism, along with his relatable style and relevant way of communicating, will make it hard for you to put this book down. Using the life of Paul and Silas, as well as with personal and engaging stories, Tim shows us how we can love God, love people, and upset the world for His Kingdom!

Chris Hodges
Bestselling author, speaker,
and Senior Pastor of Church of the Highlands

Every time we interact with someone, we make an impression on them. It's easy to get so caught up in the details of our busy schedules that we forget we are called to share the love of Jesus with every person we come in contact with. In *Upset the World*, Tim Ross gives us a beautiful picture of how we can turn someone's life upside down by showing them who Jesus is. For as long as I've known Tim, I've admired his heart for all people and his passion to share the message of love and hope that Jesus brings. This book will give you practical ways to be a light to all those around you in your everyday life. I'm so excited for you to get your hands on this book, and I know you'll be blessed as you read *Upset the World*.

Chris Durso
Lead Pastor of Saints Church

Tim Ross embodies the seemingly paradoxical combination of authentic gentleness toward people and fierce revolutionary passion toward making a difference. This book will inspire readers to see that gentleness and passion aren't optional extremes to choose between; instead, they are the necessary ingredients to trigger the real change our world desperately needs.

Mark Varughese
Senior Leader of Kingdomcity

Authors are everywhere, but voices are extremely rare. Tim Ross is an essential voice perfectly positioned for the day in which we live. And this book?! Let's just say your neighbors, friends, and family who don't yet know Jesus will thank you for reading it. *Upset the World* is guaranteed to change the way you walk OUT your walk WITH Christ.

Preston Morrison
Senior Pastor of Gateway Church

TIM ROSS

UPSET THE WORLD

GATEWAY®
PRESS

ISBN Hardcover: 978-1-951227-07-4
ISBN Study Guide: 978-1-951227-08-1
ISBN eBook: 978-1-951227-09-8

We hope you hear from the Holy Spirit and receive God's richest blessings from this book by Gateway Press. We want to provide the highest quality resources that take the messages, music, and media of Gateway Church to the world. For more information on other resources from Gateway Publishing®, go to gatewaypublishing.com.

Gateway Press, an imprint of Gateway Publishing
700 Blessed Way
Southlake, TX 76092
gatewaypublishing.com

Printed in the United States of America

20 21 22 23 — 5 4 3 2 1

www.embassycity.com
/embassyirving
/embassyirving
/embassyirving

TABLE OF CONTENTS

FOREWORD

Robert Morris

As a pastor, I've met many preachers and Christian leaders over the years, and I've discovered that you don't always have a like-mindedness with everyone you meet. Therefore, when you do meet someone who is likeminded, trustworthy, and can grow with you in ministry, it inspires and encourages you. This is how I felt when I met Tim Ross.

I first met Tim when he was a young pastor at a local church in Dallas. Since his church wasn't too far from Gateway, where I pastor, he would frequently come in as a guest speaker for our Tuesday night young adults' service. Tim later became a member of our church, and in November 2011, he submitted to the church elders his desire to plant his own church. The following year, he came on staff at Gateway in preparation for his church plant. Now Senior Pastor of Embassy City Church, Tim has grown into one of the most anointed pastors and teachers I know.

Over time, our relationship has grown closer through the faith we've placed in each other and the trust we've built. I'm honored that Tim considers me his spiritual father, and I consider it a blessing to call Tim my spiritual son. Paul told the church at Corinth, "For though you might have ten thousand instructors in Christ, yet you do not have many fathers" (1 Corinthians 4:15). While we are blessed today with many wonderful teachers and instructors, we have few spiritual fathers and mothers and even fewer spiritual sons and daughters. I am so proud of Tim and am honored to be his mentor, friend, and co-laborer in the body of Christ.

I love getting to be a part of what Tim is doing for the kingdom of God. I'm reminded of the apostle Paul's words in Philippians 2:19–23: "If the Lord Jesus is willing, I hope to send Timothy to you soon for a visit. Then he can cheer me up by telling me how you are getting along. I have no one else like Timothy, who genuinely cares about your welfare. All the others care only for themselves and not for what matters to Jesus Christ. But you know how Timothy has proved himself. Like a son with his father, he has served with me in preaching the Good News." Tim sincerely cares for the local church and continues to be an active part of our Gateway speaking team. When he preaches, I am confident he'll allow the Holy Spirit to move and that our congregation will be fed. On several recent occasions, I had to call on him with just days or even hours' notice to preach for me because I was unable to be in the pulpit. Each time he faithfully proved himself.

Tim's love for God and God's people will become evident as you read this book. I know you'll enjoy the way he communicates his heart for evangelism. The humor, winsomeness, realness, and authenticity of his words are sure to resonate with you as you learn what it means to upset the world.

There are few things more gratifying or exciting that getting the opportunity to turn someone's life upside down by sharing God's goodness and love with them. Evangelism has always been near and dear to my heart, and being able to play a part in leading countless individuals to the Lord over the years has brought me more joy than I can express. Honestly, upsetting others as the Holy Spirit prompts you to do is just about the most fun anyone can have!

I'm so excited for you to begin your own journey of upsetting the world. I pray this book will inspire and equip you to live out God's greatest commandment—to upset the world.

Robert Morris
Founding Lead Senior Pastor of Gateway Church
Bestselling Author of *The Blessed Life, Frequency, Beyond Blessed, and Take the Day Off*

INTRODUCTION

UPSETTERS

Lord, help me be an upsetter. Amen.

You may have picked up this book, read the title, and wondered, *What does it mean to upset the world?* Maybe you thought this was a book telling you how you could make the world angry; however, I think most of us can agree that we don't need a book to teach us how to do that. The world is already full of lots of angry people. To explain what it means to upset the world, we have to go back a couple thousand years.

Jesus has finished His work on the cross. He has hung, bled out, and died for our sins. He's in the tomb for three days, and then on the third day, the Holy Spirit raises His corpse from the dead. Jesus then leaves the tomb and is seen by many witnesses. He shows Himself to His disciples (who are to be His apostles), tells them He's going send them the Holy Spirit, and ascends into heaven.

And then something revolutionary happens.

The Holy Spirit starts doing extraordinary things through ordinary men and women. Regular people, like you and me, come into a relationship with Jesus Christ, are filled with the Spirit of God, and begin to go out and testify that Jesus Christ is Lord. We read about many of these amazing things in The Acts of the Holy Spirit Through the Apostles or, as it's more commonly known, the book of Acts. It's the sequel to the story of Jesus as told in the Gospels, and it tells the story of what happened *after* Jesus ascended. And unlike most sequels, it's really good!

In Acts we learn about Paul and Silas, two of Jesus' apostles, who are traveling around and telling everyone they meet about Jesus. They're preaching the gospel and baptizing people everywhere they go. They're doing incredible and miraculous things for the Lord!

Then in the sixteenth and seventeenth chapters of Acts, things get really interesting. Paul and Silas cast out a demon from a possessed slave girl. Her owner, fearing he's going to lose money, becomes so angry that he drags Paul and Silas before the city officials. They are stripped down, beaten with wooden rods, and put in prison. Paul and Silas are locked up deep inside a dark dungeon, yet instead of grumbling and complaining, they choose to pray and sing hymns to God. Suddenly a massive earthquake shakes open the prison cells, and their chains fall off. And not just off Paul and Silas but off *every* prisoner! But Paul and Silas don't do what would seem natural to most. Even though they're no longer shackled, they don't try to escape. When the jailer wakes and sees the prison doors open, he draws his sword to kill himself. But Paul shouts to him, begging him not to do it. The jailer stops, comes over to them, and asks what he must do to be saved. They reply, "Believe in the Lord Jesus and you will be saved, along with everyone in your household" (Acts 16:31). That very day, the jailer and his entire household are baptized. Then the next day, the city officials release Paul and Silas.

After spending some time with the believers in their hometown, they set out again. This time they travel through the towns of Amphipolis and Apollo, finally arriving in Thessalonica where they continue to preach the gospel.

Paul visits the local Jewish synagogue, teaching and sharing the Scriptures with anyone who will listen. He shares about his life-changing encounter with Jesus and that He is their Messiah too. Paul's teachings astonish the people! They haven't heard the gospel presented like this before, and many of the Jews, along with some Greek men and women, believe Jesus is their Messiah and become followers of Christ.

While Paul and Silas's teachings inspire many to become Christ followers, they also cause some of the local Jewish people to get really riled up! They are jealous and angry that Paul is teaching about Jesus in the synagogue. They become so angry that they form a mob and start a riot out in the streets. Determined to stop them from sharing about Jesus, they decide to search everywhere for Paul and Silas. Going from house to house, the angry mob comes to Jason's house, and thinking Paul and Silas are inside, they attack everyone in his house.

Let's just pause our story right here. It's kind of hilarious when you think about it. If you read the Bible from Genesis to Revelation, you read all kinds of crazy names, so when you get to a regular name like *Jason*, you just have to stop and smile. His name is not Abimelech. It's not Oholiab, Ahisamak, Jethro, or Methuselah. It's a random dude in the Bible named Jason. Okay, we can continue.

Once inside Jason's house, the mob can't find Paul and Silas, so they decide to drag out Jason and some of the other believers in front of the city council.

"Paul and Silas have caused trouble all over the world," they shouted, "and now they are here disturbing our city, too" (Acts 17:6).

Now, I'm a literalist, so when people talk to me, I take them literally. I have to process what they say and then try to figure out what they actually mean. It's the same way when I read the Bible. I read it literally, so when it says Paul and Silas have been causing trouble "all over the world," I take it literally to mean *all over the world.* Jesus told us the gospel will go out to "Jerusalem, throughout Judea, in Samaria, and to the ends of the earth" (Acts 1:8), but at this point it hadn't actually gotten to the ends of the earth yet. It started in Jerusalem, went through Judea, and came into Samaria. It made it to Amphipolis, and now it's in Thessalonica, *but it hadn't gone all over the world.* Yet the angry mob of people shouted, "These guys are causing trouble **all over the world.**"

In the Greek, the word *trouble* literally means 'to upset,' so the way this verse should read is "Paul and Silas have upset the world." You may think that if you've made someone upset, then you've made them angry, but the proper definition of upset is *not* to go out and make people angry. **The more accurate and appropriate definition of the word *upset* is to disturb or derange completely.** Anyone who has come into a relationship with Jesus Christ has done so because they've had their world upset—disturbed and deranged completely—by Him. He has come into your life and turned the whole thing upside down or, more accurately, right side up. An upsetter is a person who has been upset by the overwhelming love of Jesus and upsets others. The person who came to upset us is also the One who shows us how to upset the world.

> **"** An upsetter is a person who has been upset by the overwhelming love of Jesus and upsets others.

This is the message Paul and Silas shared with the world. They upset—completely disturbed and deranged—people with the message, love, and hope of Jesus Christ. And *this* is the assignment Jesus gives to each and every one of us, His believers: that we, as His sons and daughters, would upset the world with the message, love, and hope of Jesus Christ.

It's my prayer that this book will ignite you to live your life as an upsetter—a person who will go out and share the love of Christ in the most relational way possible—so you too can *upset the world*.

CHAPTER 1
UPSETTERS MUST BE UPSET FIRST

God, upset me. Amen.

My parents were vocational pastors at God's Way of Holiness Fellowship just outside of Los Angeles. Growing up, my brothers and I were at church all the time. Sunday morning, Sunday night, Wednesday night, Friday night prayer. If the doors were open, we were there.

After I graduated from high school, hanging out with my friends and going out to the clubs became my life. I was a regional performer ... okay, I was a rapper ... and I performed almost every Friday and Saturday night around different parts of Los Angeles.

I would still go to church, but it was more out of habit or obligation than relationship. After the service was over, my friends would come to pick me up, and we'd go out. It was the same routine every single weekend. They'd show up as soon as church was over, and we'd go straight to Venice Beach. After Venice Beach, we would go eat at M&M Soul Food or Roscoe's Chicken and Waffles, and after that we'd cruise Crenshaw Boulevard until two or three in the morning. Wash, rinse, repeat.

Then, on Sunday night, January 14, 1996, everything changed. I came into church, I sat in the back, and the Holy Spirit convicted me of my sins. Without a sermon or an altar call, I gave my life to Jesus. My life was completely and irrefutably upset.

As usual, my friends came to pick me up after the service. They had it timed out and knew exactly when to pick me up to go to Venice Beach. When they got there, my friend Steve came up to me, and I gave him a hug. Then I turned to my brother, Myles, who had skipped church that day, and gave him a hug. After we hugged, he looked at me and said, "Oh no! You didn't? *Did you*?" The minute I hugged him he *knew* something had changed.

When I told them what happened, Myles looked at me and said, "Oh man! You know what? I respect that. But, uh, we need to go. We'll see you later." And he shot back to the car with Steve, and they went to the beach without me.

Over the next 24 hours, my best friends became my parents, my Bible, and my PlayStation. Almost immediately, my "old" friends left me. I was *completely* alone. They were only around me for a few minutes, yet they knew something was different about me, and it was upsetting them. They weren't ready to change, so the way they dealt with it was to leave me alone. They weren't being disrespectful; quite the contrary. They were actually respecting the decision I had made.

I had fallen in love, and the moment I fell in love, *everything* changed. My life was turned upside down. I immediately stopped going to the clubs and partying. I stopped performing. I stopped cruising around with my friends. There were some things I continued to struggle with, but something immediately started changing on the inside of me. I began saying to God, "Lord, I'm in *love* with You. If that means I don't have any friends, it's okay! I just want to pursue *You.*" **Love will make you change.** If you come into a relationship with Jesus Christ but nothing about you changes, then you probably didn't really meet Him. When you fall in love and have your heart transformed, you're not relying on your will anymore; you're relying on Someone else's will. It's then that your life is completely upset. And I had been upset in the best possible way.

❝ If you come into a relationship with Jesus Christ but nothing about you changes, then you probably didn't really meet Him.

WHY BE UPSET?

If you're a Christian, it's because you've made a commitment to have your life turned upside down. The way you were living before you came into a relationship with Jesus Christ is not the same after a revelation came to you that this is not the way you should be living. Through reading Scripture and gaining an understanding of what it means to have a relationship with Jesus Christ, you found out what more than two billion people already know: your life should not be lived the way you want to live it but the way God wants you to live it. This throws the way you've been living your whole life into total chaos and disorder. It completely upsets your world.

Having a relationship with Jesus means changing your lifestyle, making different choices, replacing old habits with new ones, hanging out at new places, and, possibly, changing the people in your life. A relationship with Jesus is so completely upsetting because when He comes into your life, He completely changes you—upside down and inside out.

You might be reading this and thinking, *If a relationship with Jesus means my life and what I enjoy doing has to change, then maybe I'm not really into that type of relationship.* If you're wondering why you should give permission to God to come in and turn your life upside down, it's because He is madly in love with you. John 3:16 says, "For this is how God loved the world: He gave his one and only Son, so that everyone who believes in him will not perish but have eternal life." God is madly in love you, so much so that He sent His only Son to die so that you could live.

This may seem like Christianity 101, but it's so important for us to begin this journey with an understanding of how much God loves us. If you don't know God loves you, the way you live your life for Him will be for all the wrong reasons. If you haven't chosen to have a relationship with Him out of love, then you probably chose Him out of fear. If you're living your life this way, you'll do what God says, but you'll be doing it because you're afraid you'll go to hell if you don't obey. God is not a God of fear; He is a God of love, and He loves us in a way that is so profound it causes us to be upset.

Ephesians 1:4 says, "Even before He made the world, God loved us." This verse should make you want to have a party! Take a minute and think about this phrase: "even *before* He made the world, *He loved you.*" Before He said, "Let there be light," He loved you. Before He parted the waters, He loved you. Before He created man or woman, He loved you. Before you did anything that would disqualify you from a relationship with Him, He was already in love with you.

> God decided in advance to adopt us into his own family by bringing us to himself through Jesus Christ. This is what he wanted to do, and it gave him great pleasure (Ephesians 1:5).

God is so completely and totally in love with you that He went through great lengths to prove it. Jesus didn't wait to see if you would choose Him; He chose you first. **The good news of the gospel is before you even knew to ask the question, Christ decided to die for your sins. It's the most upsetting thing that's ever happened in all of human history.** Why should you be upset? Because Jesus died for you, and He meant to do it.

JESUS CAME TO UPSET THE WORLD

I don't know if you've ever thought about it like this, but Jesus upset the whole world. He upset it so much that we're still talking about it 2,019 years later. This man's life was so upsetting that our calendar is split *before Him* and *after Him*. It's absolutely amazing when you come to the realization that Jesus's sole purpose for coming to earth was to upset the enemy's plans for us completely. He came to bring us freedom, restoration, deliverance, healing, and power. We read about Him in the Bible, and we sing songs about Him, proclaiming His power, love, beauty, grace, and majesty. Here's the thing that's so amazing: He's given each one of us all of these same characteristics so we can upset the world. And the reason we can do it is that it happened in our own lives as well. It's because we have been upset first.

Once your life has been upset, you're going to start upsetting the world. It's going to happen naturally. Think about a time you fell in love with someone. You wanted to tell everyone, because when you're in love, it's hard to hide. It's hard for me to hide the fact that I'm married, and it's equally as hard for me to hide my relationship with the Lord. There are times I want to shout about it from the rooftops! The truth is people won't be able to stay around you for long without getting their worlds upset. It's not because you're a "holy roller" or an obnoxious religious person. It's because your life has been so overturned by what Jesus has done in you that there is no way anyone can stay around you without finding themselves being turned around and completely upset by His love. In fact, upsetting people is not just something we *should* do; it's a mandate. And the good news is we don't have to figure out how to do it alone. The person who came to upset us is also the One who shows us how to upset the world.

" The person who came to upset us is also the One who shows us how to upset the world.

JESUS UPSETS SAUL

Before Saul, which was Paul's name before he became a believer, could ever upset the world, he had to be upset first. He was born a Benjamite and was a zealous Jew who had made it his purpose in life to put an end to Christianity. And his way of accomplishing this goal was to kill as many Christians as possible. He was filled with rage and anger because so many Jews had started following Jesus, and it was threatening his religion. He was blinded by a religious spirit. (We'll talk more about "religion" in Chapter 7.) Saul's mission in life was to put a stop to Christianity, and he was willing to do whatever it took. One day, he decided to travel from Jerusalem to Damascus with the intention of going from house to house and knocking on doors to find people who were followers of Christ. His plan was to arrest them, prosecute them, and put them in prison with the hope that they'd be put to death. Essentially, Saul wanted to kill *all* Christians.

Do you realize how full of hatred and anger Saul must have been? He was so ambitious to kill Christians that he was willing to travel 225 miles to look for anyone who believed in Jesus so he could arrest them, bring them back to Jerusalem, and lock them up. I don't want to make light of the horrific nature of what he was doing, but I want to explain to you how crazy this really is. If you think about how this would play out in today's world, it would be like you flying from Dallas, Texas, to Philadelphia, Pennsylvania, looking for people who are Philadelphia Eagles fans and then arresting them, bringing them back to Texas, and putting them in jail because they're not Dallas Cowboys fans. Just imagine knocking on a random person's door to see if they're an Eagles fan and telling them they're being arrested for *not* being a Cowboys fan! It's pretty ambitious, to say the least. But this is how religion poisons the mind and leads to hate, anger, division, strife, and even death.

However, things didn't go as Saul planned. On his way to fulfill his mission, *everything* changed. Saul had an encounter with Jesus that completely upset his world. **One thing Jesus loves to upset is a spirit of religion, and that's exactly what He upset in Saul's life.** Here's how it went down:

> As he was approaching Damascus on this mission, a light from heaven suddenly shone down around him. He fell to the ground and heard a voice saying to him, "Saul! Saul! Why are you persecuting me?"
>
> "Who are you, lord?" Saul asked.
>
> And the voice replied, "I am Jesus, the one you are persecuting! Now get up and go into the city, and you will be told what you must do."
>
> The men with Saul stood speechless, for they heard the sound of someone's voice but saw no one! Saul picked himself up off the ground, but when he opened his eyes he was blind. So his companions led him by the hand to Damascus. He remained there blind for three days and did not eat or drink (Acts 9:3–9).

Scripture then says the Lord spoke to Ananias, a believer in Damascus, and told him to go to the house where Saul was staying and lay hands on him. So Ananias went and found Saul, and when he laid his hands on him, "instantly something like scales fell from Saul's eyes" (v. 18). Saul was filled with the Holy Spirit, and he "stayed with the believers in Damascus for a few days. And **immediately** he began preaching about Jesus" (vv. 19–20, emphasis added). Immediately. Not 48 hours later. Not two years later when he had a better understanding of Jesus and what happened. He didn't go to Bible school. He didn't complete a two-year discipleship program. He didn't get a bachelor's degree in theology, a master's in divinity, and a doctorate in theology. After having *this* experience, he got up, was baptized, and *immediately* started preaching that Jesus is Lord. He went from agreeing with the enemy that people should be imprisoned and murdered for believing in Jesus to being filled with the Spirit and preaching and teaching that Jesus is the Son of God. If that's not getting your life turned upside down, I don't know what is!

Saul, the man who vehemently denied the message of Jesus Christ, is no different from the people we meet today who are atheists, agnostics, or radicalized in their religion. Yet on his way to persecute Christians, he was so upset by Jesus that his life was instantaneously turned around. You see, Jesus looks for the spirit of religion, and if He finds you trying to block people from meeting Him with all your rules and regulations, you might wind up like Saul and meet Him face to face.

JESUS UPSETS PETER

While Jesus loves upsetting the spirit of religion, He equally loves to disrupt and upset people who have a spirit of independence. That's exactly what Peter is dealing with when he has an encounter with Jesus in Luke 5.

Peter is a fisherman by trade, and he has just come in from a long night of fishing in the Sea of Galilee. He and his crew worked hard, but they didn't catch anything. Now it's about midday, and he's on the shore washing his nets.

Even though this seems like a normal day, things are about to change, because today Jesus is there. Jesus has been traveling and preaching throughout Judea, and crowds of people have been following Him everywhere He goes. Today is no different. As He's preaching, the crowds begin to grow, and they press in to hear Him teach. Jesus sees two boats right on the shore that aren't being used, so He walks over to Peter and says, "Hey man, can I use one of your boats?"

Peter nods his head and replies, "Yeah, sure. I've already done my work for the night, so go ahead and use this one."

Jesus steps into the boat, and Peter pushes it off a little bit, so Jesus can preach His message to all the people without them pressing in on Him. But when He finishes preaching, Jesus doesn't get off the boat. Instead, He does something really interesting. He says to Peter, "Hey, let's go out for a catch."

Flabbergasted, Peter looks at Jesus and says, "Seriously?! You want to go out right now? You're hilarious! You show up at *my* job and try to tell me that *now* is the right time to go fishing? First You want to use my boat, but now You want to go out to the deep end of the water and catch fish? Don't You know I was fishing all night long? And we caught nothing! Zero. Zilch. Nada. Do You even know what fishing's about? Do You know how this lake works? We go out at night because the fish all come to the shallow part, and we throw out a net because the fish can't see it at night. But You want to go out in broad daylight to the deep end to catch fish when the fish can see the nets?! Are you crazy?"

I think a lot of us respond this way with different aspects of our life that we want to keep from God. The Holy Spirit gives us a little nudge, but there's an independent spirit that rises up in us, especially when we have some accomplishments under our belt.

Holy Spirit: "Hey, I want you to do this."

Us: "Hah, c'mon, man. I know what I'm doing here. I've been running this company for 20 years, and now You're trying to act like I don't know what I'm doing?"

Holy Spirit: "That's right; you don't."

When you give your life to Jesus Christ, *everything* in your life belongs to Him. This includes your business and your finances. Your life is turned upside down from what the world says is normal. **So when the Holy Spirit nudges you, you need to listen.**

> **"** When you give your life to Jesus Christ,
> *everything* in your life belongs to Him.

Against his better judgment, Peter decides to go and do what Jesus said. They go out in the middle of the day to the deeper end of the lake. They throw the nets into the deep water, and do you know what happens next? Fish fill the nets. In fact, there are so many fish that the nets begin to break! Peter has to call his friends in another boat to come help, and soon both boats are filled with fish and on the verge of sinking.

Never in all his years in the fishing industry had Peter caught this many fish. And when he "realized what had happened, he fell to his knees before Jesus and said, 'Oh, Lord, please leave me—I'm such a sinful man'" (Luke 5:8).

When you've been overwhelmed by a blessing, you can't act like you've been there before. This guy got his boat rocked, and the Bible says:

He was awestruck by the number of fish they had caught, as were the others with him. His partners, James and John, the sons of Zebedee, were also amazed. Jesus replied to

[Peter], "Don't be afraid! From now on you'll be fishing for people!" And as soon as they landed, they left everything and followed Jesus (Luke 5:9–11).

This produced absolute trust in Peter. He was overwhelmed with God's blessing, not judgment. **It's with loving-kindness that God draws people**. Peter was drawn to Jesus because he was overwhelmed with His blessing—so much so that he dropped to his knees and said, "Oh, Jesus, O Lord, I'm *so* sorry! I've never caught so many fish in all my life. You're real! You just upset my life so much. I will *never* question You again. I trust You, and I believe in You!" I wonder what would happen if this same spirit of independence was broken in us. What would happen if we gave God permission to come into all the areas of our lives that we feel like we don't want to trust Him in?

Sometimes we think we know what we're doing. Maybe you've said something like this at some point in your life: "I'm a Christian, but I don't need the Lord in my business affairs. I have my MBA, and my strategic plan is working perfectly. It's flawless! The numbers are up this year. We are doing it!" But here's what God says: "If you're going to be My disciple, you can't do spiritual things on one end and your business stuff on the other. It *all* becomes Mine. There's a new business model. No longer will you go out fishing at nighttime with *your* fishing model. Now you'll go out in the daytime and catch more fish by obeying Me." **God's way may not always make sense to us, but He wants us to trust and obey Him.** It's the only way He can break off our spirit of independence. And this is what happened in Peter's life. The spirit of independence was broken off his life, and immediately he dropped his nets and started following Jesus.

YOU MUST BE UPSET FIRST

You can't be an upsetter unless you've first been upset. Saul had a spirit of religion taken away from him when his life was upset by his encounter with Jesus Christ. Peter had a spirit of independence broken off of his life when he had an encounter with Jesus. Both men immediately began to tell others about how their lives had been upset.

There are some people who feel apprehensive about sharing their testimonies because they don't feel like they know enough about the Bible or they haven't gone to Bible school or they're afraid they'll say something wrong. But these are lies the enemy uses to keep us from telling others about how Jesus upset our lives. Let me tell you something: when the Holy Spirit reveals Jesus to you, that's all you need to begin sharing your story and declaring that Jesus Christ is Lord to the glory of God.

I'm amazed by people who think that once someone gets saved, they need to wait until they know "for sure" before they tell anyone. I've even heard people say, "Don't start telling everybody you love Jesus right away, because you don't know if you even mean it yet." That is so ridiculous! You know when you've changed and when Jesus has come into your life and upset it completely. I'm not suggesting that discipleship isn't important, because it is, or that spending time in the Word and really growing in your relationship with Him isn't important, because it is too. What I *am* saying is you don't need to wait to tell people about your experience. In fact, it's almost impossible not to talk about it! And it's because it's the best thing that's ever happened to you!

I remember calling the girl I was dating *the day* I got saved because I couldn't wait to tell her about it.

"I gave my life to Jesus. I'm so excited!" I practically screamed over the phone.

"Oh, that's cute. I get it. You love Jesus now. Don't worry; you'll be your old self soon enough." Before I could even speak, she went on to say, "It's like the time I started cheerleading. I was really excited when I made the squad, and it's all I talked about for a few weeks, but after a while it died down. And I know you're excited and all right now, but your excitement will die down too."

In the highest pitched voice I could use (because that's the voice I use when I'm happy, excited, confused, exasperated ... you get the idea), I said, "I'm sorry, did you just compare meeting Jesus to making a cheerleading squad? Because it sounded like you compared a spiritual conversion, a heart transformation, the complete freedom that I found in Christ Jesus with cheerleading. I just want to make sure I heard you correctly because I'm pretty sure it sounded like you put meeting Jesus and becoming a cheerleader in the same category. Is that what you meant when you said that? I just want to make sure. I mean, I'm breaking up with you regardless, but I want to make sure we both know the reason why." To this day, I thank God I didn't marry her.

When you've had your world upset, you go from one direction to the complete opposite direction. It's a 180-degree turn. You might not understand everything about Jesus and the Bible, and you might not have everything figured out, but *you know that you know that you know* there is no way what you experienced is hype. There is no way it's just "a feeling." When you've had your heart transformed by the power of a living God, you can rest confidently in the knowledge that your life's been upset. Something has been overturned. Generational curses have been broken. You are now under the Holy Spirit's conviction. Those bad thoughts and habits you never felt guilty about, you suddenly realize you shouldn't be doing them anymore. The off-color jokes you laugh about with your friends at work suddenly don't seem so funny. It's because your world has been upset in the biggest way possible!

Saul began teaching and preaching immediately. Peter began following Jesus and teaching immediately. They didn't wait. And you shouldn't either. Don't be afraid to tell people what God has done in your life.

UPSETTERS LOVE JESUS

The reason you can't upset the world until you've been upset is that **upsetters love Jesus**. I'm not talking about the zealous type of love that jumps up and down on couches shouting, "I'm in love with Jesus!" Or the overly spiritual person who every time you ask him how he's doing says, "Bless God, I'm highly favored of the Lord! I'm the head and not the tail, above and not beneath! I've got everything going on in Jesus' name!" I'm talking about the type of love that is intimate, that is personal, that is deep, that is reverential. I'm talking about a love that leads to faithfulness and fidelity in Jesus Christ. I'm talking about a love that makes you change from where you live because you've fallen in *love* with Jesus. I'm not talking about the cultural Christian Jesus. The necklace with the sparkling rhinestone cross around your neck. I'm not talking about having a tattoo of Jesus. I'm talking about when you're all alone, when you have a moment in the morning, afternoon, or evening and you think, *I'm so in love with Jesus that I have to spend some time with Him. I must be in His presence. I have to read His Word. I'm passionately in love with the person who saved my soul, made me whole, and caused me to change. There's no way I would have done this on my own. Something had to have happened to my heart because things that I would never be convicted of, I'm now convicted of. Things that I would never be concerned about before, I'm concerned about now. I used to think* *that going to church was crazy, and now I find myself in there every single weekend. I thought people who read the Bible were weird, and now I'm reading my Bible every single day.*

Love does crazy things to you, and the reason why an upsetter can't be an upsetter without loving Jesus is because only people who are in love are infectious. People only follow people who are really passionate about something or someone. People who are not passionate about things don't have people follow them. But if you are passionate about something, people will follow your passion.

" Only people who are in love are infectious.

Here's a thing about the Kingdom that's so amazing: the whole thing is upside down. When we fall in love with Jesus, we become so passionate about Him that it makes people ask, *"You*? You love Jesus? Well, maybe there *is* something to it." That's why I love the redemptive story of Christ in everyone's individual way. Every person who gives his or her life to Jesus has the opportunity to shock other people who would *never* believe that you gave your life to Jesus.

Jesus wants to upset your life. If you haven't been upset by Jesus yet, will you let Him upset you today?

CHAPTER 2
UPSETTERS LOVE PEOPLE

Holy Spirit, help me love people so I can upset them. Amen.

Years ago, my friend Janette got me a job as a temp at JWT Specialized Communications in Los Angeles, a leading advertising agency in the US and one of the largest in the world. That is where I first met Mary (not her real name). She was a little lady, *maybe* five feet tall without her heels. She might have been 4'11". But despite her small stature, we always knew when she arrived at the office because we could hear the sound of her footsteps as she walked down the hallway.

CLOMP! CLOMP! CLOMP! CLOMP!

I don't think she put sound effects on the heels of her shoes to give them such a robust sound, but I wouldn't have been surprised to find out that she did. Every single day when she walked into work, we heard this sound.

There was something else unique about this little lady: she wasn't nice! In fact, Mary was as mean as they come, and she was a clock-watching micro-manager. If you went to lunch at 12:00 pm, you better be back at 12:59 and 59 seconds. If you weren't, she'd know about it and would not hesitate to write you up!

Everybody was scared of Mary. If anyone was chatting with a co-worker or taking a break and heard the sound of her footsteps (or footclomps!), they'd immediately jump back into their work and look super busy, even if they weren't. I noticed this happening a lot when I first started working there, so one day I asked Janette about her.

"I've noticed everyone gets so scared and stressed out when they see Mary. Why is everyone so scared of such a sweet, little lady?"

Immediately Janette snapped back at me, "She is *not* sweet! She's a horrible human being!"

It was obvious Janette had had some unpleasant interactions with her that had left Janette feeling a little wounded. But as she continued to share with me why this woman was so terrible, I heard the Lord telling me we needed to go after her. Janette was a believer, and I knew there were several other believers in the office too. So with the Lord's prompting, I decided we needed to do something.

"You're looking at what she's *doing*, but I'm looking way past that," I said. "I think we should go after her."

Janette looked confused and asked, "Go after her? Do you want us to jump her after work? What are you saying?"

"No, that's not what I mean at all. I don't want to beat up a person who is barely five feet tall as she's trying to leave work. We should go after her because we don't wrestle against flesh and blood. We can go after her, and she doesn't even need to know it. We can start by praying for her and praying over this office. Let's get here early over the next few days and pray. Let's ask God to start breaking some things up in her life and see if it works. Are you with me?"

We started meeting the very next week to pray. We'd get to the office early and walk around and pray for her, for other people in the office, and for the atmosphere. After a few days, I started taking a little bit of olive oil with me and dabbing it on everybody's seats. I wasn't pouring oil all over the seats or leaving any stains. I was using just enough to anoint them as we prayed. However, I did mess up one time when I didn't get the oil to heat ratio right. I climbed up onto the copy machine so I could reach Mary's door and put some oil on it. She had a really tall door, and as I was standing on the top of the copy machine, I had to get up on the tips of my toes so I could put a little cross over her door with the oil. I don't know if the heat up there made the oil spread, but it just started pouring down. It was ridiculous! As I was cleaning up all the streaks of oil on the top of her door, I remembered she was barely five feet tall and would never see it.

We continued to pray every morning that week, but by Friday afternoon, nothing had changed. I'm sure you're thinking, *You were doing so much praying! Surely you were going to have a breakthrough!* Um, no, she was still stomping. And she was still mean.

We decided to continue meeting to pray the next week. And here's what happened. (I promise, I couldn't make this up if I wanted to.)

Monday: CLOMP! CLOMP! CLOMP! CLOMP!

Tuesday: CLOMP! CLOMP! CLOMP! CLOMP!

Wednesday: CLOMP! CLOMP! CLOMP! CLOMP!

Now, I don't know what happened between Wednesday and Thursday, but something changed.

Thursday: Clomp. Clomp. Clomp. Clomp.

It was easing up!

Friday: Step. Step. Step. Step. Step.

It was unbelievable! We didn't even know she had gotten to work on Friday! Everyone was looking around and asking, "Is she here? Have you heard her yet?" But no one had heard anything! The fact that she stopped stomping around the office would have been enough of a breakthrough, but then she took it up a notch.

Mary came out of her office at noon and asked us, "Does anybody want pizza for lunch? I'm buying!" She bought pizza for the whole office! In just two weeks, people were thinking, *Who are you?!*

The best part is that at the end of our third week of praying for her, Mary started *asking us* to pray for her! It wasn't long before she and Janette became close friends and started going to Bible study together.

We had completely upset this little lady's world! And the way we did it was by deciding to *love her*. Even the meanest little lady we'd ever met couldn't escape being upset. Too many times, we choose to stay away from mean people or people who make us feel uncomfortable. We play it safe by associating only with people in our nice little Christian clique at the office. Maybe we even intentionally stay away from people who are different from us or who don't love Jesus. But think about this: how is God going to do it without you? Why would you deny them the very Light they need to see Him? Because the truth is, they won't see Him unless they see Him in you. If you're huddled in the corner with all your "nice" and "safe" Christian friends, others won't have the chance to see Him. Quite honestly, we spend a lot of time talking to each other before we talk to God. I think if we talked to God first, we would have less to say to each other about how different we are and more to say about how we're alike.

> **" They won't see Him unless they see Him in you.**

LOVE EVERYBODY

This is one of the most racially charged, politically crazy times our country has ever seen. People are mad at each other based on what they post on social media or what their bumper sticker says. It's so easy for us to get angry and worked up by people who have a different opinion than ours. We need to take all that passion and hostility toward people and turn it into love for others. You need to love them, because if you don't love them, then His Kingdom can't come to them. Let me put it another way: **if you're mad at somebody, you will also be mad at Jesus.**

In Matthew 5:43–48, Jesus says:

> You have heard the law that says, "Love your neighbor" and hate your enemy. But I say, love your enemies! Pray for those

who persecute you! In that way, you will be acting as true children of your Father in heaven. For he gives his sunlight to both the evil and the good, and he sends rain on the just and the unjust alike. If you love only those who love you, what reward is there for that? Even corrupt tax collectors do that much. If you are kind only to your friends, how are you different from anyone else? Even pagans do that. But you are to be perfect, even as your Father in heaven is perfect.

You see, upsetters love people. *All* kinds of people. They even love people who have different political views. They love people who hate them and people who despise them. Upsetters love people who are unlovable. They love *everybody*. But as we talked about in the last chapter, **you have to love Jesus first. It's the *only* way you can love people who don't love you.** If you're only praying for people who are amicable to you, who like you, who respond well to you, then you're *never* going to advance His Kingdom. Unless you start targeting people who are a little bit obstinate, who are rude, who don't like you that much, who have anger issues, who need an attitude adjustment, you're never going to be a real upsetter.

" Upsetters love people who are unlovable.

As a believer, you're an ambassador of Jesus Christ. Through Him, you have the power to change the atmosphere. And the way you do that is by taking on the mind of Jesus and saying, "I'm just going to love everybody the same way You did." It doesn't mean you have to like what they're saying or doing, but you do have to love them right where they are. You have to die to your will and respond with the nature and character of Christ Jesus.

Jesus disturbed the religious atmosphere everywhere He went, and He did it by loving people. Every time He went to a city, He would do great deeds for people who were disenfranchised, sick, or poor. He was just nice to people, even those who didn't seem to warrant such generosity. The only people who had a real problem with Jesus were the religious people, and it was because He was doing things that didn't fit in their religious box. It didn't fit with what had been written for them in the Mosaic Law, which they had been practicing, rehearsing, and memorizing for literally thousands of years.

One of the best examples of this is in Luke 10:25–37 where Scripture tells us about a religious expert who approached Jesus and asked, "How am I supposed to have eternal life?" Now before I tell you how Jesus responded, I want you to understand what a religious expert was. In this context, a religious expert was the equivalent to a lawyer. He wasn't just a person who went to church and studied the Bible. He was a person who was considered well-versed in the Torah, understood the context of the Old Testament, and would debate anybody who didn't see the Scriptures in the same way he did. And much like an attorney, when he asked Jesus this question, he already had the answer in his mind.

Have you ever had a conversation like this with someone? They ask you a question, but they already know where they want you to go with the answer. There's a little bit of sauce in their tone when they ask, "You're not going to wear *that* shirt, are you?" or "Did you *really* like that movie?" I usually respond to questions like this with, "Well, based on your tone, I can tell *you* didn't like it!" This is how it was when the religious expert asked Jesus, "Teacher, what should I do to inherit eternal life?" (Luke 10:25). He knew what he thought the answer was and wanted to hear what Jesus would say.

And I love Jesus' response. He said, "Why don't you tell Me how *you* see it? You're the legal dude in the room, so why don't you tell Me how you interpret it?"

"Well, I'm supposed to love God with all my heart, all my soul, all my strength, and all my mind. And I'm to love my neighbor as myself."

What's interesting about the religious expert's response to Jesus is that he was talking about securing eternal life, yet he was actually piecing together two Old Testament Scriptures. He first quoted a portion of the Shema, which is Deuteronomy 6:4–9. He quoted verse 5 when he said, "You must love the Lord your God with all your heart, all your soul, and all your strength." Then he added Leviticus 19:18: "Love your neighbor as yourself."

Much to the religious expert's surprise, Jesus agreed! "That's exactly right! If you do this, you'll really live!"

Jesus was saying that if you really love God with all your heart, all your soul, all your strength, and all your mind, you will be living the life you were called to live. And if you love your neighbor as yourself, it just gets *even more* enjoyable. It doesn't mean there aren't going to be people you have problems with or oppositions against. But if you do the first thing, the second thing becomes something you *can* do. If you really love God, then you *can* love your neighbor.

It's impossible to love—really love—people out of our own emotional wealth of happiness and generosity. **It's only an overflow of our relationship with God that makes it possible to deal with people and love them.** And not only the kind of people you tend to like or gravitate toward but also the kind of people you don't.

But the story doesn't end there. The religious expert decided to test Jesus further. When he quoted Deuteronomy 6:5, the man was referring to his fellow Israelites, people who were just like him. Ready for a debate over this loophole, he asked Jesus, "And who is my neighbor?" (Luke 10:29).

Not willing to be drawn into a debate, Jesus answered his question with a story about a Jewish man who was making the treacherous journey from Jerusalem to Jericho (Luke 10:30–37). The distance between these two cities was more than 18 miles with a 3,300-foot descent in altitude. Not only was it a long and difficult walk, but it was also littered with bandits who were trying to take advantage of people and rob them. As he was walking, the man was pummeled by bandits who stripped him, beat him, and left him half dead on the side of the road.

As he was lying there, a priest walked up and saw him. Instead of helping the man, though, the priest crossed to the other side of the road and kept walking. He literally passed him by. Let me just stop here and say Jesus is setting up a brilliant story. This guy was half dead on the side of the road, and out of *all* the people He could have said came by, Jesus chose a priest. He could have chosen a tax collector, a guy who worked in the local market, or a rich, Roman centurion. But Jesus said a *priest* came by. In other words, a senior pastor just happened to be walking down the street on the same day this dude got the snot kicked out of him. And the senior pastor looked at him, but because he was in a hurry and had to get to his church service that started at 10 o'clock, he went to the other side of the road and kept walking.

Now, here's the thing that baffles me. I've read commentaries that seem to justify the priest's actions. One of them even said a high priest couldn't touch a dead body because it would make him ceremonially unclean and not allow him to go to his place of worship. While that's true, there's one problem. The man was *not* dead; he was half dead, which meant he was also half alive. Consider how many people don't want to deal with people's issues because they only look at their half-dead side and not the other side that's still alive. And Jesus said that's exactly what this priest did; he went to the other side of the road and kept walking.

Then Jesus rubbed it in a little more and said a temple assistant—the senior pastor's associate pastor—walked over, *looked* at him, and then crossed to the other side of the road and kept walking. Once again, Jesus didn't choose to use a regular Jewish guy; He chose the second in command of the church. And what he did was actually worse than the priest, because he walked up to the man and was close enough to see him wounded and battered almost to death, yet he still chose not to do anything about it. This sounds a lot like religion. (We'll talk more about how much Jesus hates religion later in the book because there's a lot to unpack.) In the end, both men were close enough to see what the situation was, but they chose to honor their religious rules rather than get involved.

Here's where the story gets really good. Jesus decided to throw a grenade and blow up this man's religious thinking. And it wasn't just any grenade, nor just any explosion. It was a frag grenade, so chunks were flying out of it that were meant to rip into all of the religiosity for anyone and everyone within earshot of where Jesus was speaking. Here's what He said:

> Then a despised Samaritan came along, and when he saw the man, he felt compassion for him. Going over to him, the Samaritan soothed his wounds with olive oil and wine and bandaged them. Then he put the man on his own donkey and took him to an inn, where he took care of him. The next day he handed the innkeeper two silver coins, telling him, "Take care of this man. If his bill runs higher than this, I'll pay you the next time I'm here" (Luke 10:33–37).

Are you kidding me? A despised Samaritan! The priest didn't stop to help. The temple assistant barely slowed down before he crossed the road to leave. But the Samaritan not only stopped and helped him, but he also took his oil and wine and began nursing the Jewish man's wounds right there on the side of the road. Then he went a step further by taking him to safety and paying for a nice room in an inn so he could recover in comfort. The Samaritan even told the innkeeper, "Hey, if this is not enough money, I'll settle the debt when I come back in town. Just keep him here until he's feeling better."

This story is so crazy! While it may not seem alarming to you, to the man Jesus was talking to, it was shocking. It was very strategic for Jesus to use a Samaritan man as an illustration in his story because during this time Jews *hated* Samaritans. When Assyria overtook the region of Israel and colonized it, many of the Israelites who lived there married the Assyrians in the region of Samaria. So Samaritans were half-Assyrian and half-Israeli. Essentially, they were biracial.

I often wonder what story Jesus would have told to ruffle our feathers and get us upset in 2019. It would be just like Him to say, "A man was beaten up and left for dead on the side of the road, and a republican walked by but then kept on going. Then a democrat walked over to him, but she didn't stop either. Instead, she turned around and went the other way. But then, a despised communist walked up to the guy and showed him compassion and took care of his wounds." This is the kind of stuff I love about Jesus. He throws stories like this out there and gets people upset. He may not be walking on the earth today, but He's still doing it.

The story ends with Jesus asking the man, "Now, based on everything I just said, which of these three do you think was the neighbor?" This man's religiosity must have been choking him. Can you imagine the look on his face as Jesus asked this? But Jesus wouldn't let up. He was going to make this man say the Samaritan was the neighbor! The Samaritan was the one whom this man was supposed to love as much as he loved himself. It was fantastic! The religious leader kind of choked and said, "The one who showed him mercy." He couldn't even say the name "Samaritan." And Jesus ended the conversation, "Yes, now go and do the same" (v. 37). This man believed he should love only his fellow Israelites and was trying to trap Jesus into saying something contrary to the Torah. But this was actually worse than he could have ever imagined because Jesus just told him to go and be like a *Samaritan*!

What is Jesus after? **He wants us to love people. And that means *everybody*!** Most of us have some people group we despise. It may not even be at a conscious level; it may be subconscious. It may be a way you were raised or the way you were taught or the way you've been conditioned. Whatever it is, something in our culture is shaping you to despise people. This spirit of division has a lot of names, and the prevalent one in the United States is racism. As believers, we have to understand this is just a spirit of division. Sadly, this isn't just an issue outside the Church. It's inside the Church too. And the *only* way to defeat it is through love. I'm talking about a deep kind of love. You love Jesus enough to allow Him to come for the stuff on the inside of you that blocks you from genuinely *loving* people whom you would normally despise.

WHEN WE LOVE GOD, WE CAN LOVE PEOPLE

There are people I know who love the Lord, but they tell me they're not a "people person." Remember, I'm a literalist, so when people say this to me, it always blows my mind! I think, *You're a "people." Does that mean you don't like yourself?* The truth is, if you love God and obey His commandments, then you're going to love people. You can't be an upsetter and not be a "people person."

> **❝** If you love God and obey His commandments, then you're going to love people.

There are people in our own families whom we would despise if not for the love of God. It has to happen in you regardless if it happens in them or you will be in bondage for the rest of your life. Remember what Jesus told the religious expert? "Hey, if you do this, you will live your best life. You will actually enjoy life! But if you choose not to do these two things, you will live life, but you won't enjoy it." Instead of reading books or listening to podcasts and messages about how God wants you to live life to the fullest and how He wants to bless you so you can prosper, start actually putting it into practice. Don't just read and listen to the Word; do what it says.

If you work hard and earn a million dollars, but you're still mad at everybody you meet, you're not going to find pleasure or satisfaction in life. If you have a Gucci bag, Coach loafers, and drive a Lamborghini, but you won't stop and pick up the bloodied person in the street because you're racing to get to church, you are not going to enjoy life. If you don't love God, you won't love people, and if you don't love people, you can't upset them.

A natural byproduct of loving God is becoming friendly, and friendliness upsets people's lives. When God starts really washing you through and through, you start becoming nicer and kinder. It's a result of being free. When I meet people who aren't nice, I know they're not free. They may not be bound in sin, but they're definitely not free. Think about it like this. Have you ever watched someone come out of the restroom with toilet paper stuck to the heel of their shoe? They may not be stuck in the bathroom, but they're not totally free from where they came. You may not be in complete bondage, but you're not completely free because you still carry evidence of where you've been.

When you love God, you also start doing good deeds for people. Proverbs 11:30 says,

The seeds of good deeds become a tree of life;
a wise person wins friends.

I don't know many mean people who win a lot of friends. I just haven't seen it. **When you're friendly, you don't have a lot of enemies.** Proverbs 16:7 says,

When people's lives please the Lord,
even their enemies are at peace with them.

What is an enemy? An enemy is someone whose goal is to harm you. When we love God, it's hard for our enemies to be real enemies because we disrupt them so much with His loving-kindness. By loving them, we make it almost impossible for them to hate us.

When we love God, we become faithful not just to Him but also to the teachings of Jesus. John 8:31 says, "Jesus said to the people who believed in Him, 'You are truly my disciples if you remain faithful to my teachings.'" It's easy to recognize disciples of Jesus Christ by how closely they endeavor to stick to Jesus' teaching even when it goes against their feelings. I've never met a disciple of Jesus Christ who, at some point, didn't disagree with something Jesus told him or her to do. I can't say it enough: Jesus upsets people everywhere He goes. He did it when He was here on earth, and He is still doing it today. It's easy to recognize who His disciples are because they are the ones who decided to do what He said even though they didn't agree with Him or think it made sense.

Our church, along with many others, participated in Revive Texas a couple of years ago. For 50 days, in 10 regions across the Dallas-Fort Worth Metroplex, believers joined together and hit the streets to share the gospel and make disciples. In those 50 days, 2,685 people gave their lives to Jesus Christ. We just went out and talked to people and were nice and friendly to them and shared our stories about how Jesus had upset our lives. One day when the group was getting ready to go out, they were all praying about where they should go. One of the ladies looked up and saw a woman full of tattoos on the street. She heard the Lord tell her to give that woman a hug. So right in the middle of the prayer, she walked over, gave her a hug, and said she loved her. Being friendly and showing this woman how much she was loved opened the door for this lady to share about the Lord.

We need to be available to meet people where they are. Too many people believe the lie the enemy has placed in the world that Christians are hypocrites and don't really care about people. "They're just judgmental and hateful." Let's prove them wrong by showing people how much we love them. Love was Jesus' motivation to upset the world, and it should be ours too. Jesus came to upset the world, and if we're going to be more like Jesus, then we need to be upsetting people.

> **"** Love was Jesus' motivation to upset the world, and it should be ours too.

Several years ago, a local LGBTQ group called the church where I was serving and said they were coming to picket and protest that weekend. Our security team met with us before the weekend to prepare us for what we should expect and how we should handle the situation. They wanted to make sure the congregation and the staff were safe and protected. They explained that anyone can show up and protest, but they're not allowed on the property, and they're required by law to stay back a certain distance.

That weekend everyone on staff was on high alert. No one said this out loud, but it seemed as if everyone was thinking,

"The gays are coming! The gays are coming!" It was almost like we were waiting for a bomb to drop. We had been briefed and were ready to jump into action if anyone crossed the line and tried to come into the church to cause problems.

As we got ready for the service to begin, I asked one of the guys on the security team, "Where are they going to be protesting?"

"Well, if they come, they're going to be over here at this corner," he said, pointing across the street.

"Can we get some Danishes and coffee in case they do show up? I want to go out there and give them some refreshments and hug them!"

"Would you really want to do that?" he asked, seeming genuinely shocked.

"Why wouldn't we? We're a church, and we love people. The best way to break down this wall of hostility is to show them how much we love them. I might as well go out there and give them some Danishes and burst their mindset by showing them how well we love. Oh, and if it keeps raining, I want to give them some of our umbrellas and make sure they don't get wet."

Sometimes we get so worked up over people who are not like us or people who have different beliefs than we have that we forget (or choose not) to love them. But it's love that's going to upset their worlds. And if we can't love them, they're never going to have their lives upset.

The group never showed up to protest, but if they had come that day, I was ready for them! My arsenal was full of Danishes, coffee, umbrellas, and all the hugs they could handle. I was fully prepared to go out there and show them how much we loved them.

I think God used that situation to show us how backward we'd gotten things. We said we loved them, but we weren't *showing* them how much we loved them. Our words weren't lining up with our actions. What we needed to do was to step out of our prayer circle and go pray for them. We needed to stop what we were doing and give them a Danish and a hug. The truth is it's hard to hate up close. You have to be far away to hate. When you're up close to someone, showing kindness and loving them, their mindset begins to change. **Only love can burst the mindset of hate.**

From that day forward, we began to view those who came against us differently. Instead of looking for ways to avoid conflict, we chose to look for ways to love them. While that particular group didn't come protest that day, there have been others who have shown up during our weekend services. And when they did, they were met with refreshments, cold bottles of water, hot cups of coffee, and of course, lots of love and plenty of hugs!

One of the foundational Scriptures of this book is Proverbs 25:21–22:

> If your enemies are hungry, give them food to eat.
> If they are thirsty, give them water to drink.
> You will heap burning coals of shame on their heads,
> and the Lord will reward you.

You might be shocked at the reason why this is a foundational Scripture. After all, this is a book about sharing the message, love, and hope of Jesus in a relational way. To get a better understanding, let's look at how I literally read this verse: "If my enemy is hungry, I feed them. If my enemy is thirsty, I give them something to drink. When I do these things for my enemy, God rewards me. But that's not all He does. He also heaps shame upon them like burning coals, and I get to hear their scalps sizzle." [Insert maniacal laugh!] I get to burn my enemy's scalps and hear them sizzle just by being nice to them? And I get rewarded for it? Yes, please! This is how you upset the world with the message of love and hope. That's it. Everything else we do is built on top of that.

When we treat people who come against us with kindness and love, the Bible says, "The wicked will see this and be infuriated" (Psalm 112:10). They become upset when we're nice! Not because we're walking around with picket signs and joining in protest movements, but because of our generosity, our good works, and our *love* for others. I'm sure you've heard the old saying, "Kill 'em with kindness." That's exactly how we're going to upset the world. If we love God, we'll love people. And if we love people, we're going to upset the world! It's that simple.

I have three aunts who are lesbians. All of them are incredibly loving women, but one of them was especially kind and patient with me as a young boy. She even endured my storytelling. Growing up, I loved writing and illustrating comic books. These weren't just thin, little 20-page comic books; no, they were the size of novels and had sections and chapters. Now, I wasn't the greatest illustrator, but my storytelling was on point. I remember a time when I was around 10 years old that my aunt came over to our house, and I gave her one of my comic books to read. She was so encouraging to me, commenting on how my drawings were so creative and my stories were interesting and well-written. I remember her telling my dad, "He's so talented! This boy is a genius!" She was always nice, kind, and encouraging to me. I liked her and felt good around her because of the way she treated me. It wasn't until I was about 20 years old that I found out she was in a relationship with another woman. While I don't condone this lifestyle, I don't despise my aunt. I love her. I love all my aunts. I just don't agree with their lifestyle.

If I allow a religious perspective to seep into my heart, I will *only* love other people who are believers like me. Guess what? You *can* love people who aren't like you. You *can* love people who have different lifestyles than you. In fact, it's the only way you're going to be able to upset them. You can't upset people you despise, but you can pray for people you love. You can even pray for them without them knowing! You can pray for them just like we prayed for Mary. You can pray and put a whole host of angels on them. You don't have to get into an argument with them. It's okay if you disagree with the choices they're making. It's also okay to despise their sin, but you *cannot* despise the person. You have to love them. And you can do it because when you're faithful to Jesus' teachings, you'll want to be faithful to loving others. When you do this, you will upset people.

> **"** You can't upset people you despise,
> but you can pray for people you love.

We need to become fearless in our faith. We need to say, "This is where I stand. You may not agree with it, and that's okay. We don't have to agree, but this is where I stand, and I'm not moving from this spot. It doesn't mean I don't love you. In fact, it means I love you in spite of our differences." Hug people. Have conversations with people and build deep relationships with them. We don't have to agree with everything going on in their lives, but here's what we can't do: we can't leave people on the side of the road bleeding. **Life is too hard already for the body of Christ to walk past people who are broken, hurting, and in pain—emotionally, spiritually, physically, and psychologically.** We can't continue to do it. If you can't love people right where they are, you probably have a hard time receiving love from God. The truth is hurt people hurt people. But the good news is free people free people, and upset people upset people. You can't help but upset people when you've had your life completely overturned. You can no longer act like nothing happened to you.

What are you going to allow God to do through you? Are you not giving yourself permission to love people because you despise them? Take an inventory of your heart. Who is the enemy setting you up to despise? It could be somebody in your family. It could be a neighbor. It could be an ex-boyfriend or ex-girlfriend. It could be another church member. It could be the Church. This I know for certain: if you don't resolve this issue in your heart, the enemy will make sure that person or those people continue to be what keeps you from living life to the fullest. But the good news is that if you love God, you'll love people. And when you love people, you'll upset them, because love upsets the world.

CHAPTER 3
UPSETTERS NEED THE HOLY SPIRIT

God, thank You for sending the Holy Spirit
to upset me. Amen.

T here was a show that aired on MTV in the early 2000s that documented a celebrity's life and was narrated by the celebrity. The person on the show always began their story with, "You think you know ... but you have no idea." When it comes to what you heard about the Holy Spirit as you were growing up, I think He'd say to you, "You think you know ... but you have no idea."

So let's start with a basic introduction. The Holy Spirit is God. That's who He is. He's not the side person in the Trinity. He's not like the "bonus Jonas" brother. He's not extra. You can't take Him or leave Him. It's not God the Father, God the Son, and then this random guy you can choose or not choose to incorporate into your life if you want to, but if you don't, it's okay. No, He *is* God. He is part of the Trinity: God the Father, God the Son, and God the Holy Spirit. And like the Father and Jesus, the Holy Spirit is a *person*, not some crazy ghostly power. He's God. If we can't upset the world without the Father and Jesus, then we certainly can't upset the world without the Holy Spirit.

HE LEADS US INTO TRUTH

The Holy Spirit didn't come to draw glory to Himself. He came to lead us into the truth. Truth isn't a philosophy or an ideology. **Truth is a person, and His name is Jesus.** Jesus said of Himself, "I am the way, the **truth**, and the life" (John 14:6, emphasis added). When the Holy Spirit leads people into truth, He's leading them to a person. He's leading them to Jesus.

The Holy Spirit is the *only* person who brings people to Jesus. This means we can't upset the world without the Holy

Spirit. I know this is going to mess up the minds of people, especially pastors and evangelists, who like to say, "I win souls to Christ" (Proverbs 11:30). Um, no you don't. Many people have erroneously taken a very simple verse from the book of Proverbs out of context and tried to take credit for leading people to Jesus. However, that's not what this verse means. Better translated, this passage means a person who knows how to win friends is wise. You can be friendly without knowing Jesus. But the credit cannot be attached to a person on earth if someone comes to Jesus. It's only because of the Holy Spirit.

Now, here's what's amazing. Jesus took something as simple as communicating the gospel and decided to use that, along with the Holy Spirit's power, to bring people to Him. I've never met anyone who was eloquent enough or charismatic enough on their own to bring someone to the Lord. I could never preach a message or share something powerful enough to make people believe in an invisible being. I alone don't have that kind of power. It's *only* through the Holy Spirit that people come to the Lord. We must have the power of the Holy Spirit working in us to lead people to Christ. He's the one doing the work, not us. We're just the vessels. **If we're going to upset the world, the Holy Spirit has to go with us.** And the only way He can go with us is if He's living inside of us. The good news is that if you can say Jesus is Lord, then you have the Holy Spirit!

❝ It's *only* through the Holy Spirit that people come to the Lord.

If I haven't convinced you yet that it's not what we preach and teach that brings people to Jesus, then let me show you what the Bible has to say. Paul, the most scholarly person in the New Testament, calls preaching "foolishness" (1 Corinthians 1:17–18). And there's a reason why he calls it that; it's because it is. It shouldn't work. But there are a lot of things God does that shouldn't work.

- God used people blowing trumpets to bring down the walls of Jericho.
- God used an ox goad in the hand of Shamgar to defeat the Philistines.
- God used a young shepherd boy, a slingshot, and five smooth stones to defeat the giant Goliath.
- God used a man to hold out his staff to part the Red Sea so the Israelites could walk on dry ground, and then He had the man move his staff so the sea would close and drown the entire Egyptian army.
- God used a jawbone of a donkey in the hand of Samson to overthrow an entire army.
- God used a big fish to get the attention of Jonah.
- God used a young virgin to give birth to the Savior of the world.
- God used a boy with a few fish and loaves of bread to feed more than 5,000 hungry people.
- God used His one and only Son, Jesus, to upset the world.

None of it makes sense! But God uses things that seem foolish in our eyes to bring glory to Himself. And it's because there's a more powerful person at work behind all of these things: the Holy Spirit.

HE TEACHES US AND REMINDS US

> But when the Father sends the Advocate as my represen-
> tative—that is, the Holy Spirit—he will teach you every-
> thing and will remind you of everything I have told you
> (John 14:26).

There's only one reason why we have the Gospels (Matthew,
Mark, Luke, and John). It wasn't because the disciples had impec-
cable memories. It's because they spent time in the presence
of Jesus, and after His death, resurrection, and ascension,
something amazing happened. The Holy Spirit reminded them
of *everything* Jesus said.

John lived the longest of all the disciples. By the time he was
in his 80s or 90s, all of the other disciples had died of old age or
had been killed. It was then the Holy Spirit had John write about
Jesus' time on earth. Can you imagine what John might have
said? "Man, I'm 90 years old! I don't know if I can remember
everything. My memory is kind of hazy." And the Holy Spirit
said, "Don't worry! I'm going to remind you of *everything* Jesus
said and did. All you have to do is write it down."

This is still true for us today. The Holy Spirit reminds us
of the things Jesus said, but the only way He can remind us
is if we read His Word. The Holy Spirit can't remind us of
something we don't know. It has to be *in your mind* before you
can be *re*minded. When you read the Bible and spend time
learning it and studying it, the Holy Spirit will remind you
of the things you read. So when you're sharing about Jesus
with someone, and you need a Scripture, the Holy Spirit will
remind you of the right one. He'll tell you what to say. You
may even wonder, *How did I remember that?* It was the Holy
Spirit reminding you of His Word. If you put His Word in
your heart, He will bring it to your remembrance. You don't

have to be a Bible scholar or remember exactly where every-thing is in the Bible. But you do have to open up the Word of God and read it. Then when you need it, the Holy Spirit will remind you of what Jesus said. (And Jesus isn't just in the New Testament. Jesus is in the Bible from Genesis to Revelation.)

I've met with people in counseling sessions who tell me about a situation they're going through, and I'll ask them, "Do you have a word from the Lord to stand on?" And they almost always innocently retort, "Well, that's why I've been coming to church. I want to receive a word from the Lord." The truth is, you can receive a word from the Lord every day. You don't have to wait until you're in a church building or with a pastor. Your ears don't have to itch that long. You can open up your Bible anytime, anyplace, and receive a word.

The disciples spent time with Jesus, and we can too. If we want to have the same type of experience the disciples had with Jesus, we just need to *read* the Word of God. If you want to know what He has to say to you, pick up your Bible and read it. Read it every day. When you do, the Holy Spirit will give you great understanding and clarity, and when you need it, He will remind you of what it says. As upsetters, we need to know the Word of God so the Holy Spirit can bring it to our minds when we need it.

So many people hear all about the Holy Spirit's power and His gifts, but they don't know who He is as a person. Yet when Jesus talked about Him, He talked about who He is as a person. He didn't tell us how He has nine gifts He gives the body of Christ. He didn't talk about the power He gives us to do miracles and healings. And do you know why? Because Jesus wants us to enjoy the Holy Spirit and be in love with Him for who He *is*, not for what He does.

" Jesus wants us to enjoy the Holy Spirit and be in love with Him for who He *is*, not for what He does.

Many people who have a background in a denomination where they only teach about the power of the Holy Spirit tend to only talk about—and only want—His power. Sadly, they don't know Him as a person and aren't in love with Him. The problem with this perspective is the power and the person are two different things. **The Holy Spirit is a person *who has power*.** I can always tell when someone only wants the power but not the person, because they are enamored with the gifts but not the character.

There are also people who want the Holy Spirit's power, but they're not nice. They are mean, rude people. I see why some people are scared of Spirit-filled churches. They go to church and see people raising their hands and dancing in worship and "Amening" the message, but they are just mean and rude. The parking lot person was mean, the ushers were mean, the praise and worship leader screamed for 30 minutes. Then the preacher got up for 45 minutes and told them how they're all going to hell, then started ranting about something on television, then told them what club not to go to, and ended the message by asking, "So who wants to know Jesus? Who wants to be filled with the Holy Spirit?" Um, not me! If that's what the Holy Spirit is like, I think I'll pass! Their character doesn't reflect the Holy Spirit. Their meanness causes people to wonder, *Is Jesus really here in this church? Because He's not with these people!* If the Holy Spirit is your dear friend, you should look like Him. I'm not saying you have to be perfect, but there's no way you can have a vibrant relationship with the Holy Spirit and be mad and rude all the time. Who cares if you can speak in tongues if you're mean in English?!

As upsetters, we should look and act like the Holy Spirit. We should allow Him to mold us and change us into the image of Jesus more and more every day. Maybe when you first got saved you were mean, but if you're still mean and rude five years later, you're not allowing Him to change you. It's the Holy Spirit who changes us from the inside out. It's the Holy Spirit in us that's going to attract people to us, and it's the Holy Spirit who's going to bring them to Jesus.

HE TESTIFIES

The Holy Spirit testifies about Jesus, and He can do that because He was and is with Him. Romans 8:11 tells us, "The Spirit of God, who raised Jesus from the dead, lives in you." This is so powerful! The Holy Spirit, the one who raised Jesus from the dead, lives in *you*! Jesus said, "I'm sending you the Holy Spirit, and He's going to testify about Me. And the reason He can testify about Me is because He's the one who has been with Me this whole time." He testifies that it was a virgin birth because it was through Him that Mary conceived. He testifies that Jesus actually did the miracles we read about in the Bible because He's the one who made them happen. He testifies that Jesus rose from the dead on the third day because He's the one who got Him up. And Jesus says this same person lives in each one of us! It's absolutely incredible!

Jesus couldn't have done any of the things He did on His own. It was only because He was filled with the Spirit. He was filled with the Holy Spirit from his mother's womb, but because He was in a human body, He was limited to the same parameters we're limited to. Some people like to think that when Jesus was on earth He was like Superman and flew around the world saving people. The truth is, He couldn't do anything in

His earthly ministry without depending on the same person He's telling us to depend on. It's the reason why we must have the Holy Spirit if we're going to upset the world. Before Jesus ascended into heaven, He went to His disciples and said, "You've been with me and have seen all the things that have happened, but I'm going to leave to go be with my Father. And when I leave, I'm going to leave you with the Person who was doing all these things in this body, because you won't be able to do any of the things I've done without Him." If Jesus needed the Spirit of God, don't you think we need Him even more?

Jesus sent the disciples out to perform miracles through the power of the Holy Spirit. They weren't doing it on their own. The Spirit went with them and performed these miracles on their behalf. Here's what Jesus says in John 14:15–17:

> If you love me, obey my commandments. And I will ask the Father, and he will give you another Advocate, who will never leave you. He is the Holy Spirit, who leads into all truth. The world cannot receive him, because it isn't looking for him and doesn't recognize him. But you know him, because he lives with you now and later will be in you.

Think about this: When the Holy Spirit was *not* indwelling the disciples, they were able to do some pretty cool things, *but* they were still cowards. It wasn't until the Holy Spirit was *inside* that things started to change. (We'll unpack this more in the next chapter.) Once they had His power, the disciples could do the things Jesus did. You see, there's not one miracle that Jesus did that did not require the Holy Spirit's assistance. The Holy Spirit was *always* present. He's the one who allowed Him to do *everything* you read about in Scripture (John 16:13–15). In the same way Jesus needed the Holy Spirit, we need Him to upset the world. **If you're going to upset people, the Holy Spirit needs to go with you.**

" There's not one miracle that Jesus did that did not require the Holy Spirit's assistance.

HE CONVICTS PEOPLE OF SIN

God sent the Holy Spirit to represent Christ's interest on earth. As our Advocate, the Holy Spirit is also like a lawyer who gives counsel and protects us. When Jesus says, "I'm sending the advocate to be my representation," here's what He's saying: "I have to go away but don't worry. Your legal counsel is coming. The Father is sending the greatest lawyer who has ever been, and He's going to be the one who leads you and guides you into all truth." The Holy Spirit is here to protect Jesus' followers by giving them their rights. It's what lawyers do. They show up, and they speak on your behalf.

Have you ever heard someone say, "Sir, I refuse to talk until I have legal representation"? Take a moment and think about whatever trial or circumstance the enemy has been trying to get you to respond to. Now, here's your response: "I refuse to talk until my legal representation shows up. I am *not* going to talk until the Holy Spirit gives me a word about this situation. Once He shows up and gives me a word, I will repeat that word. I don't want to give an emotional answer; I want to give God's answer."

When the disciples went out to upset the world after Jesus ascended to heaven, they were not alone. The Holy Spirit was with them and gave them the words to say. In the same way, He gives us the words we need to say. He will come to you from the Father and testify about Jesus. And when the legal representation shows up, here's what He says: "You don't have the right to remain silent. You have the right to speak as a diplomatic citizen of heaven. Your Dad opened His mouth, and everything was. Now you have to open your mouth and confess." That's why it says in Romans 10:9, "If you confess with your mouth the Lord Jesus and believe in your heart that God has raised Him from the dead, **you will be saved**" (NKJV, emphasis added). Why is there an attachment there? Luke 6:45 says, "For out of the abundance of the heart his mouth speaks" (NKJV). When you believe in your heart and confess with your mouth, then you are saved.

In John 16:8, Jesus says this about the Holy Spirit: "And when he comes, he will convict the world of its sin, and of God's righteousness, and of the coming judgment." Did you get that? *He will convict the world of its sin.* Not me. Not you. Him. It's not me going down the list of all the sins you can ever do and hoping you feel bad about it. No. It's the Holy Spirit who convicts people of their sins.

I taught a series at church about giving our tithes to the Lord, and during the message the Holy Spirit started convicting a guy in the congregation about a lifestyle he was in that wasn't pleasing God. I wasn't even talking about purity or living morally. I was talking about giving, but the Holy Spirit convicted him of his immoral lifestyle. After the service, he came up to me and said he wanted to have a conversation with me because he was being convicted of an immoral lifestyle and wanted to know what to do about it. I'm sure the look on my face threw him a little. If he could have heard my thoughts, he would have heard, *"Really?!* Because I was just talking about giving. But you're standing here telling me you need to repent because you're living in sin?!" But that's how the Holy Spirit works. I didn't have to be in the pulpit saying, "Hey you! You're shacking up! You're out there having sex and doing all sorts of crazy stuff. You're going to hell if you keep living in sin!" I simply delivered the message the Lord gave me, and the Holy Spirit did the rest. After we talked and prayed, the guy made a decision to come out of that immoral lifestyle and walk with the Holy Spirit with a renewed commitment and devotion to God. It's not our job to convict people of their sin.

The Holy Spirit convicts the world of its sin, and He does a way better job at it than we could ever do.

The Holy Spirit doesn't convict us of our sins just when we first get saved. It's not a "one and done" thing. It's not as though you gave your life to Jesus, and all of the sudden you're not convicted anymore. It's ongoing. And He's good at it because He lives in you. **You can fool people you don't live with, and you can even fool people you do live with, but you can't fool the person who lives *in* you.** The Holy Spirit shows people the real nature of their sin, the truth about righteousness found only in God, and the coming judgment. He's the one who convicts the world of its sins. If you're praying for a loved one, keep praying for them and loving them; then sic the Holy Spirit on them! You don't have to confront them or say to them, "I can't believe you're doing this! You're breaking God's heart." Just love them where they are, and then go sic the Holy Spirit on them. He will convict them of their sin.

HE TELLS US WHAT JESUS IS SAYING NOW

I've been teaching about the Holy Spirit for over 20 years now, but while I was researching and preparing to write this book, I received new revelation. It lit me up! John 16:13 says, "When the Spirit of truth comes, he will guide you into all truth. He will not speak on his own but will tell you what he has heard. He will tell you about the future." Now, a lot of people think this verse has to do with prophecy, so they show up to church looking for a breakthrough and want the Holy Spirit to give them a word for their life. But the Holy Spirit doesn't want us to wait until we can get to church. The verse says He tells us about "the future." That could be Sunday, or it could be tomorrow. If we wait until we get to church on Sunday to hear from Him, we could miss what He wants to tell us right now. Jesus didn't say, "Come to church, and you will get a word." He said He's going to talk directly to *you*. God doesn't want you to get dependent on a preacher. He wants you to come to Him, and He'll reveal it to you through the Holy Spirit. He wants to talk to you personally. We show up to church so we can be in community with each other, not so we can become dependent on the pastor for a word. **You should grow in the Lord and be dependent on the Bible, not on a pastor or leader, to give you a word.** Pastors don't have any superpowers. The Lord doesn't love me more because I'm the pastor of a church. He wants to speak to each and every one of us about what's going on in our lives, and He wants to do it at any time and any place.

Let's look at the rest of that Scripture in John 16:

> He will not speak on his own but will tell you what he has heard. He will tell you about the future. He will bring me glory by telling you whatever he receives from me. All that belongs to the Father is mine; this is why I said, "The Spirit will tell you whatever he receives from me" (vv. 13–15).

The Holy Spirit tells us what Jesus is saying. I just want you to think about this: God is on the throne, and Jesus is at His right hand. I don't know how He does it. Maybe He leans over and says, "Hey, Holy Spirit, go tell Crystal not to quit that job." "Hey, Holy Spirit, go tell Bobby to forgive his dad. Tell him it's not worth it to hold a grudge." If we want to know what Jesus is saying, we need to listen to what the Holy Spirit says to us.

> **❝ If we want to know what Jesus is saying, we need to listen to what the Holy Spirit says to us.**

The Holy Spirit wants to talk to you about your life *right now*. While He does give people prophetic words for you, He also wants to talk to you about things that are going on now. And why wouldn't you want to listen? *He knows everything!* How many times have you thought, "If I'd only known …"? You can know because the person living inside of you knows, and He wants to talk to you and tell you things. And here's how you know the Holy Spirit is speaking to you: if it works out, it was the Holy Spirit. If it doesn't work out, that was you. Don't blame it on God when you do things on your own that the Holy Spirit isn't telling you to do.

Sometimes the Holy Spirit wants to talk to us about the regular, everyday stuff in our lives. When I first moved from California to Texas and got my own place, I was feeling mighty! Before I went to rent my apartment, I went over my budget and knew what my expenses would be, so I was prepared to ask for the smallest apartment available. But when I got there, the apartment manager informed me that all the small apartments were sold out or occupied. She could give me the next one up, but it was bigger and more expensive. This would have made my budget *very* tight. I could swing it, but I would be eating turkey with no bread—just straight protein. I decided to leave and think about what I wanted to do. After some thought and going over all the details, I decided to go back and rent the bigger apartment. I met with the same lady, told her I wanted the bigger place, and she began to get the paperwork ready. "Sign here, initial here, here, and here …" The usual rigmarole. As we were doing this, the Holy Spirit said to me, "Hey, ask her about the smaller apartment." And I immediately shot back (in my mind), "Nah, I'm good."

Isn't this what we tend to do with the people who are closest to us? Your friend tries to give you advice, but you say, "No, I'm good. I know what I'm doing." The truth is your friend is only trying to help you. It's the same way with the Holy Spirit.

So the Holy Spirit and I started going back and forth. And He said again, "Ask her about the smaller apartment." And I said, "No. Listen, I was just here two days ago, and they were all filled. Do I really need to remind you about this?"

The difference between arguing with the Holy Spirit and my best friends on earth is I would probably argue with the latter for 15 minutes longer. Even though I know the Holy Spirit *knows* what's available, because I'm so familiar with Him, like I am with my friends, I don't always listen to Him the first time. (Or the second or third times!)

I told Him no again. "She's already printed out all the forms and contracts. I don't want her to have to do more paperwork for me." I told myself I was just trying to be polite, but truthfully, I was a people pleaser back then and didn't want to bother her or stress her out. (I've since been delivered from that! Praise Jesus!)

But the Holy Spirit is relentless. "Ask her about the smaller apartment." He had to tell me *three times* to ask her about the apartment!

Finally, right before I signed on the last line, I said, "I hate to ask you this, but um, is the smallest apartment available?" I didn't have much confidence the answer would be yes.

She perked up and said, "I can't believe you asked! Just this morning a guy called and said he has a friend who lives in this complex, and he's going to room with him. So, yes, a smaller apartment just became available this morning! In fact, they're cleaning it right now. Do you want to go ahead and get that apartment?"

"Yes!" I said with excitement and a newfound confidence that comes only from the Holy Spirit.

She ripped the old paperwork up, got the new paperwork ready, and I was in! And she wasn't even upset I asked.

Jesus is still on the throne, and He cares so much about me that He made sure I got an apartment I could afford. Let that sink in. The King of the universe, the one who died for my sins, cared about which apartment I lived in! It's mind-blowing, but it's also what's so awesome about Jesus. He cares about the smallest of details in our lives. He cared so much that He leaned over and said to the Holy Spirit, "Hey, I need Tim to get that smaller apartment. Tell him to ask her for it." That's what the Holy Spirit does—He tells us what Jesus is saying *right now*. Jesus bends down and whispers in the Holy Spirit's ear, and then He tells us. We just need to be willing to hear Him and obey what He says. And thankfully, He puts up with a very stubborn Tim Ross who likes to argue with Him. I'm thankful He keeps speaking to me and doesn't give up!

Maybe you need Jesus to bend down and whisper in the Holy Spirit's ear about a situation in your life. Maybe it's something you're going through with a friend or a co-worker. Maybe you need Him to tell you how to reach the person who refuses to go to church with you. Maybe you need Him to tell you whom He wants you to upset with His gospel message. Whatever it is, He's ready and willing to speak to you about what's going on in your life right now.

CHAPTER 4
UPSETTERS AREN'T IN CONTROL

Holy Spirit, I submit my will to Yours.
Change me. Amen.

W hen I go to the food court at the mall, I never take the free samples. I think it's weird when I see someone standing around with a tray waiting for people to pass by so they can stop them and ask, "Do you want to taste one of our nuggets?" And many times, it feels more like they're shoving food in my face than handing it to me. Maybe it's paranoia on my part, but I'm freaked out by those little samples. Quite honestly, free food scares me a little bit. My first thought is always, *Why is it free? If the food at your restaurant is that good, I'll just pay for it.* I'm not willing to put something in my mouth simply because a nice person is handing it to me on a little toothpick. Um, no. That's just weird.

This is the same way I felt when I gave up my life to Jesus Christ, and people began trying to shove the Holy Spirit on me.

People would say, "You need to be filled with the Holy Spirit!"

I'm like, "Oh, okay. Why?"

"You just do!"

Flashback to the food court, you basically just put the Holy Spirit on a toothpick and shoved Him in my face. My first reaction is, "No sir, I don't need this. And why are you so angry? If He's someone who's supposed to help me, He sure made you mad. I don't want the Holy Spirit if He's anything like you." They could never explain to me who He is, what He does, or why I needed Him. All they could tell me is that I had to have Him.

We already learned that we need the Holy Spirit if we're going to upset the world, but you need to know *why* you need Him. You need to know who He is and what He does, because if you haven't been Spirit-filled, you may feel a little bit like I did when I first got saved.

There's a misconception that when someone gives their life to Jesus Christ, they are automatically filled with the Holy Spirit.

This has caused a lot of confusion, theological angst, deliberation, and debate among Christians about whether or not someone is Spirit-filled when they give their life to Jesus Christ or they have to receive the Holy Spirit later. Scripture is very clear that when someone gives their life to Jesus, it's because the Holy Spirit *brought* them to Jesus. However, Scripture is also clear that Jesus has reserved the right to baptize people *into* the Holy Spirit. These are two very different things.

We're going to look again at the verses in John 14, but this time we're going to focus on the end of the passage. Jesus has already sent His disciples out to perform miracles through the power of the Holy Spirit. Let's be clear: they weren't doing these things on their own. Jesus gave them the Holy Spirit, and the Spirit went with them and performed these miracles on their behalf. And here's what Jesus says to His disciples:

> If you love me, obey my commandments. And I will ask the Father, and he will give you another Advocate, who will never leave you. He is the Holy Spirit, who leads into all truth. The world cannot receive him, because it isn't looking for him and doesn't recognize him. But you know him, because **he lives with you now and later will be in you** (John 14:15–17, emphasis added).

What Jesus is saying is, "You know Him, you've talked about Him, you've seen His power, and He's with you right now. But He's not *in you* yet. I have not yet been glorified, and I have not baptized you *in* the Holy Spirit."

A great example of this is in Acts 19:1–2:

> While Apollos was in Corinth, Paul traveled through the interior regions until he reached Ephesus, on the coast, where he found several believers. "Did you receive the Holy Spirit when you believed?" he asked them.

"No," they replied, "we haven't even heard that there is a Holy Spirit."

This doesn't show up until the nineteenth chapter of Acts. Pentecost has already happened, and the Holy Spirit has already come on the people who were up in the upper room. Now those people are going out and declaring the gospel. And here we are *19 chapters deep* into the book of Acts, and we read about Paul traveling through the interior regions until he reached Ephesus on the coast where he found *several believers*. And here's what he asked them: "Did you receive the Holy Spirit when you believed?" Now, if they had already received Jesus, shouldn't they already have the Holy Spirit? Then why is Paul asking this question? It's because the Holy Spirit can be *with* you but not *in* you.

There are a lot of people in churches today who would have the same response these people had—"No, we haven't even heard that there is a Holy Spirit." I've met people who have grown up in church their whole lives, but when I talked to them about the Holy Spirit, their response was, "*Who*?" They knew all about God the Father and God the Son, but God the Holy Spirit was never talked about in their church. They were told to stay away from "that guy" because everybody who gets with Him is crazy. He makes people do crazy things and tear stuff up.

> "Then what baptism did you experience?" [Paul] asked.
> And they replied, "The baptism of John."
> Paul said, "John's baptism called for repentance from sin. But John himself told the people to believe in the one who would come later, meaning Jesus" (Acts 19:3–4).

❝ The Holy Spirit baptizes us *into* the body of Christ, but it is Jesus who baptizes us *into* the Holy Spirit.

As soon as they heard this, they were baptized in the name of the Lord Jesus. Then when Paul laid his hands on them, the Holy Spirit came on them, and they spoke in other tongues and prophesied. There were about twelve men in all (Acts 19:5–7).

They believed in Jesus—they were Christians—but they were not Spirit-filled. Then Paul prayed for them, the Holy Spirit came on them, and they were filled. That word *on* can also mean *in*. They were in-filled with, or baptized in, the Holy Spirit, and this is Jesus' assignment for all of us as upsetters. Remember, John 14:17 says, "He is the Holy Spirit, who leads into all truth." So as we learned in the last chapter, when He leads us to the truth, He's leading us to Jesus.

Jesus baptizing us into the Holy Spirit can be found in *every single Gospel*. The first three Gospels—Matthew, Mark, and Luke—are synoptic, or similar, Gospels. John's Gospel is different from those because Matthew, Mark, and Luke only covered the last year of Jesus' earthly ministry. John covered His *entire* earthly ministry. Also, Matthew's Gospel and John's Gospel are eyewitness accounts—the writers were there with Jesus. Mark's Gospel and Luke's Gospel are accounts from other people who were with Jesus. It's like an investigative journalist going out and saying, "Oh, I heard you were there when the riots took place. Could you tell me what happened?" That's how they got their information. But even though Matthew, Mark, Luke, and John were written from the two eyewitnesses and two people who heard about it, they all said that John the Baptist said the same thing!

I baptize with water those who repent of their sins and turn to God. But someone is coming soon who is greater than I am—so much greater that I'm not worthy even to be his slave and carry his sandals. He will baptize you with the Holy Spirit and with fire (Matthew 3:11).

I baptize you with water, but he will baptize you with the Holy Spirit! (Mark 1:8).

John answered their questions by saying, "I baptize you with water; but someone is coming soon who is greater than I am—so much greater that I'm not even worthy to be his slave and untie the straps of his sandals. He will baptize you with the Holy Spirit and with fire" (Luke 3:16).

I didn't know he was the one, but when God sent me to baptize with water, he told me, "The one on whom you see the Spirit descend and rest is the one who will baptize with the Holy Spirit" (John 1:33).

It's in all four Gospels. You only need two witnesses for agreement. In 2 Corinthians 13:1, the apostle Paul writes, "In the mouth of two or three witnesses shall every word be established" (KJV). Yet God wants to make it so clear to us that He puts it in the Bible *four* times. I think He did a good job of establishing that Jesus baptizes us in the Holy Spirit.

I've given all this context so you'll have an understanding of why we need the Holy Spirit. Once you understand who the Holy Spirit is and what He does, all fear and anxiety about Him will be eliminated. Scripture is very clear, especially in the book of Proverbs, that it's important to have understanding. Proverbs 3:13 says,

Joyful is the person who finds wisdom,
the one who gains understanding.

And Proverbs 8:9 says,

My words are plain to anyone with understanding,
   clear to those with knowledge.

I could list at least 25 more verses like this. The simple truth is if the people telling me about the Holy Spirit when I first got saved had an understanding and could have explained why I needed to be filled with Him, I wouldn't have felt like they were forcing Him on me. If we're going to upset the world, it's important not only to understand why we need the infilling of the Holy Spirit, but we also need to be able to explain Him to others and tell them why they need to be filled with Him too.

UPSETTERS NEED TO BE FILLED

Now that it's been established who He is and what He does, I want to share with you why we can't upset the world without Him, and the best way for me to do that is by using vodka. But before we go there, let's look at Ephesians 5:18: "Don't be drunk with wine, because that will ruin your life. Instead, be filled with the Holy Spirit." Why would Paul, of *all* the analogies he could make on the infilling of the Holy Spirit, use getting drunk with wine? At first glance, it's shocking to think that his comparative analysis to being filled with God the Holy Spirit is getting drunk with wine. But the reason he uses this is that alcohol has a counterfeit effect on your life, in your body, and in your system from that of the Holy Spirit. What Paul is actually saying is, "You don't have to do it *that* way. You can do it *this* way. Don't get drunk with wine. Get drunk with something good—the Holy Spirit."

To really understand this, let's take a closer look at the word "filled," which is a verb used with an object. In this case, we are the objects, and the Holy Spirit is the One who fills us.

Definitions give us clarity and context, so let me give you the eight definitions for the word "filled."

1. To make full; put as much as can be held into.
2. To occupy to the full capacity.
3. To supply to an extreme degree or plentifully.
4. To satisfy fully the hunger of; to satiate.
5. To put into a receptacle.
6. To be plentiful throughout.
7. To extend throughout; pervade completely.
8. To furnish with an occupant.

When we get filled with the Holy Spirit, this is exactly what happens. He fills us—the receptacles—to full capacity and an extreme degree, satisfying us fully by being plentiful throughout and pervading completely. But there's one more thing He does, and this may be the most important: **the Holy Spirit moves in and occupies a place in our lives.** He comes in and says, "Hey, I've watched you trying to live your life the way you wanted to for a long time, but you're terrible at it! So, if it's okay with you, I'm just going to move in here and start running things. See, if you get full of Me, I can handle all that stuff that you haven't been able to handle. You know those things you've been losing your mind over? I can give you God's mind on things, and everything will come together."

We need to be filled with the Spirit—not just any spirit but the Holy Spirit. When I explain the Holy Spirit to people, I like to use vodka as an example. I can say without hesitation that there's not one person reading this book who can be drunk with—or filled with—the contents of an entire bottle of vodka and stay the same person. You would change, even if you didn't want to and even if you tried your best not to change. The spirit that's in a bottle of vodka *will* change you. It makes really quiet people loud and really loud people louder! But more than that, it changes the way you walk. It changes your character.

> **❝ We need to be filled with the Spirit—not just any spirit but the Holy Spirit.**

This is why police officers use field sobriety tests to determine if a person is drunk with a spirit. Let's say someone is drinking and driving, and they get pulled over by a police officer. When he comes to the window and asks if they've been drinking, their speech almost immediately gives them away: "No, offisher, I not drinky anyting."

Then the officer says, "Please step out of the car. I have a very quick way to determine if you're under the influence. I don't even need to give you a breathalyzer test. I just want to see you walk. I'll know if you're under the influence of a spirit because it will change the way you walk."

So they get out of the car and walk in what they think is a straight line, but it's very clear to the officer that they're not sober (because they're walking in circles). They are obviously under the influence of a spirit.

Being filled with the Holy Spirit also changes the way you walk. Here's what Paul was saying to us: "Don't get drunk with that spirit. Get drunk with the Holy Spirit. He can do the same thing the spirit in the bottle can do, except He does it in a completely opposite way. You won't walk crooked; you'll actually walk straight. You'll be a different person if you let the Holy Spirit fill you. You've been trying to walk on your own, and you get kind of sideways and can't stay on the line, but don't worry! We all miss the mark, and I understand that. But if you live your life Spirit-filled and Spirit-led, you will be walking in a straight line. And when you start to get off the line, the Holy

Spirit will say, 'Hey, you're off the line,' and will gently guide you back." When you're filled with the Holy Spirit, He will change you from the inside out and line up your character with His.

Being filled with the Spirit also changes the way you talk. It changes your conversation. I grew up in a Pentecostal church that was very charismatic. I love the Spirit-filled movement, I love Pentecostal churches, and I love charismatic churches. However, when I talk about the Holy Spirit changing the way you talk, the first thing most people with a background similar to mine think about is speaking in tongues. People will often say that if you don't speak in tongues, you're not Spirit-filled. Truthfully, I've seen a lot of people speak in tongues, and I question if they're really Spirit–filled. To be clear, I'm not talking about a prayer language; although, I think everyone has the ability to pray in a heavenly language. I'm not talking about the gift of tongues, which will be a different known language on earth (1 Corinthians 13:1). I'm not even talking about a heavenly language where the Holy Spirit prays for you (Romans 8:26–27). I'm literally talking about your conversations with people. The things you talk about with other people changes when you're filled with the Holy Spirit.

If you get filled with vodka, your conversation changes too. And, quite honestly, sometimes it sounds a lot like speaking in tongues. If your uncle got *completely* filled with a spirit like vodka, he might sound like this: "Heeeeeeeyyyyy!!!! You gottag-ottalotta you hondacar overthar car drives. Hahahahaha!! Yamember thatttt?" Your drunk uncle is in the living room speaking in "tongues," and your auntie says, "Oh, he's talking about cars and what happened when he was a teenager. Don't even mind him." Only your auntie has the interpretation, because he's filled all the time!

But when you're filled with the Holy Spirit, He gets to govern what you say before you even say it. He's the quality assurance check on what comes out of your mouth. The Holy Spirit comes on the inside of you and *instantly* changes the way you talk. He changes the way you speak to other people, even the way you talk to your spouse.

This is how a conversation with the Holy Spirit might go once you've allowed Him to come inside and fill you.

You: "I'm so mad at my wife! She's going to hear it today. She can't do this to me! It's *my* money."

Holy Spirit: "You won't talk like that to My daughter."

You: "Oh, that's right Holy Spirit, You're living *in* me! But if I don't say something, she'll think she won this argument. I can't let her win."

Holy Spirit: "Why are you thinking about winning? You have an issue with pride."

You: "Um, yeah, I'll just stop right now."

Holy Spirit: "Here's what you will say, and here's how you will say it."

The things you talked about and the way you talked before you were filled with the Spirit will change. You won't even have a desire to talk the way you did before, because being filled with the Spirit changes your conversation. Scripture tells us a great way for you to know if someone is Spirit-filled. Galatians 5:22–23 says, "But the Holy Spirit produces this kind of fruit in our lives: love, joy, peace, patience, kindness, goodness, faithfulness, gentleness, and self-control. There is no law against these things!" Here's what this verse is saying: **"When you get filled with the Holy Spirit you should be loving, joyful, peaceful, patient, kind, good, faithful, gentle, and have self-control."** That's what it looks like to be Spirit-filled.

If you're a believer and you've already been filled with the Spirit, you may need a refill. Acts 2 is when the Holy Spirit fell, but by Acts 4, the believers were asking for refills. I don't know if it was 3 days or 7 days or 14 days, but they couldn't go a couple of weeks without needing a refill of the Holy Spirit to give them what they needed to go back out and declare Jesus Christ with boldness. This is why, as upsetters, we not only need to be filled with the Spirit, but we also need to be refilled with the Spirit. It's not a one and done thing. **You need to ask for a daily portion of the Holy Spirit to come on the inside of you to make it through the day.** It needs to happen early, and it needs to happen often.

Being filled with the Spirit also changes the way you act. It changes your conduct.

In drinking circles, spirits are often referred to as "liquid courage." They're called this because when a mild, docile, and very standoffish person gets too much spirit in them, they get bolder and braver than they've ever been before. The way they act when they're filled with the spirit is very different from how they conduct themselves in their everyday lives. It gives people so much "courage" that a person who's only 5'1" might walk up to someone as tall as Shaquille O'Neil who's 7'1" and pick a fight. Why did their conduct change? They got filled with a spirit, and it changed the way they act.

The same is true for us when we're filled with the Holy Spirit. When the Holy Spirit is in you, it makes it difficult to walk away from your relationship with Jesus, because He's there *with* you. Every time the enemy tries to lure you with a temptation or a negative thought, the Holy Spirit is there to say, "You don't have to believe that. You know that's a lie." But if you don't let the Holy Spirit come in and change you from the inside out, it's easy to go back to your old lifestyle and habits.

John 21 gives us a clear picture of what it's like when we aren't filled with the Spirit. After Jesus died on the cross, the disciples (the ones who have been mentored by Jesus to upset the whole world) were locked in a house and were not going to come out. Essentially, they said, "We're done. We're just going to stay in this house." Then Peter said, "You know what? I'm going fishing. I'm going back to my previous job before I got into this relationship with Jesus Christ. I'm going back to my *old* lifestyle." It's evident the disciples hadn't been filled with the Spirit yet, because when you're filled with the Spirit, you're not the same person. You won't have a desire to go back to the things you did before. It's hard to move out of a relationship with somebody when He's living in you.

All throughout the Gospels, the disciples were cowards, but by the time you get to the end of the Gospels, you see they have become incredibly bold people, almost overnight. And it's because they were filled with the Holy Spirit. He was *in* them. In Acts 4:1–22, we read about the time Peter and John were confronted by the priests, the captain of the Temple, and some of the Sadducees. These leaders were very disturbed, or *upset*, that the disciples were teaching people that through Jesus there is a resurrection of the dead, so they arrested them. The next day, Annas the high priest and Caiaphas (the same two guys who put the hit on Jesus) interrogated the disciples:

> [They] demanded, "By what power, or in whose name, have you done this?"
>
> Then Peter, **filled with the Holy Spirit**, said to them, "Rulers and elders of our people, are we being questioned today because we've done a good deed for a crippled man? Do you want to know how he was healed? **Let me clearly state** to all of you and to all the people of Israel that he was healed by the powerful name of Jesus Christ the Nazarene, the man you crucified but whom God raised from the dead" (Acts 4:7–10, emphasis added).

The members of the council couldn't believe what they were hearing! "Are these the same guys who were with Jesus? And is this the same man who denied Jesus three times before He died? What happened to him?!"

I'll tell you what happened to Peter—he got filled with the Holy Spirit, and it changed his conduct. It changed the way he responded to the issues that were going on in his life. He suddenly had a boldness and courage that he didn't have before he was filled.

If we're going to upset the world, we must be filled with the Holy Spirit. He has to be in us for us to have the boldness and courage to upset people. The apostle Paul writes in Romans 8:11,

> The Spirit of God, who raised Jesus from the dead, lives in **you**. And just as God raised Christ Jesus from the dead, he will give life to your mortal bodies by this same Spirit living **within you** (emphasis added).

Christ's resurrection is the most upsetting thing that has ever happened in all of human history. And who did it? The Holy Spirit—the One who raised Jesus from the dead.

" If we're going to upset the world, we must be filled with the Holy Spirit.

This understanding of being filled with the Spirit may be new to you, and you might be thinking: *Tim, are you saying that when I'm filled with Holy Spirit, I have to let Him control my life? Well, I don't like not being in control.* To put it bluntly, you need to get over it, because that's exactly what I'm saying. If we're going to be upsetters, we need to get used to not being in control. When someone is drunk with a spirit, they're *not* in control, and the spirit makes them do crazy things. In the same way, when someone is filled with the Holy Spirit, they're not in control, and the Spirit makes them do crazy *and* amazing things! Things they could never have done without Him.

This is why the comparative analysis Paul uses is so brilliant! Wine will make you drunk and give you courage, but it's a cheap imitation. The Holy Spirit will do the same thing, but He's the real deal. He will change your behavior. He will change the way you walk. You won't be stumbling around. You will walk upright with integrity, character, and morals. He will change the way you talk and the conversations you have with people and what you talk about. You won't want to gossip or spread rumors anymore. And you don't need to be scared of Him. He likes you a lot! In fact, He likes you so much that He wants to live on the inside of you and fill you completely.

If you let the Holy Spirit fill you, He'll completely change your life. And the good news is you can receive the Holy Spirit at any time. You don't have to wait for a church service or for someone to come to your house and pray with you. Jesus wants to give you the gift of the Holy Spirit right now. All you have to do is have an open heart to receive Him. It's that simple.

❝ If you let the Holy Spirit fill you, He'll completely change your life.

CHAPTER 5
UPSETTERS AREN'T RELIGIOUS

Lord, help me not to be a religious hypocrite. Amen.

I hadn't been saved 90 days when I started attending a Bible study at a new church. At the beginning of the meeting, everyone went around the room and shared a little bit about themselves. I told the group how excited I was because I had just gotten saved! The leader looked at me and said, "Do you speak in tongues? Because if you don't speak in tongues, you're not really saved." This was so confusing to me because I believed in my heart, beyond a shadow of a doubt, I was saved. When I stood up that day in church, I was fully convicted of all my sins, I repented, and I asked Jesus to save me. I knew it was true. But as sure as I was that I was saved, I was just as certain I didn't start speaking in tongues or receive a prayer language that day.

As I was thinking about what he said, another one of the guys in the group looked over at the leader and sheepishly said, "Well if that's true, I've never heard my grandmother speak in tongues, and she's a devout woman of God. Are you telling me she's not saved?" Exasperated, the leader threw his hands up in the air and said, "Well if she doesn't speak in tongues, she must *not* be saved!"

I didn't know what to think about what this guy was saying. But I knew someone who could help me sort it all out—my momma. My momma is one of the wisest women I know, and she knows the Bible inside and out. She is the person I would go to whenever I had questions. I would lie down on my momma's bed, lay my head on her lap, and ask her questions about the Bible. Once I got comfortable, I said, "Mom, I had a guy tell me tonight at Bible study that if I don't speak in tongues, I'm not saved. Is this true?" And as soon as it came out of my mouth, my momma said, "Uh-uh, that's not the truth at all! Baby, you were saved the moment you gave your life to Jesus. Whether you speak in tongues or not, *you* have a relationship with Jesus

Christ. That man lied to you. Do not believe anything he said." That's all I needed to know.

The truth is this guy was hung up on religion. He had been taught in his church's denomination that unless you spoke in tongues, you weren't saved. **But the truth is salvation is based on** *relationship*—**a relationship between you and Jesus Christ.** This guy had a religious spirit and was basing salvation on a religious to-do list.

RELIGION VS. RELATIONSHIP

There's been a lot of talk over the last decade about religion versus relationship. I've heard many people say, "I don't want anything to do with religion. I just want a relationship with Jesus." I understand what they're trying to communicate, but the truth of the matter is we're all religious. There's nothing inherently wrong with religion. In fact, most of us have some religious proclivities. We're religious when we go to church every single weekend. If we have a consistent prayer life or devotion time, we have religiously carved out some time to be in the presence of God. If I go to Salt Grass Steak House, I will religiously order the carrot cake. There's nothing wrong with some religious tendencies. The problem comes in when religion is what motivates us. We need to ask ourselves, *Are we being motivated to serve the Lord by religion? Or are we being motivated by our relationship with Jesus Christ?*

Jesus knew the religious leaders of His day were being motivated by the wrong reasons. They weren't serving God out of a relationship with Him. Their motivation for abiding by the law in the Torah was selfish and self-serving. That's why some of the most scathing remarks Jesus gave about religion in all of the New Testament were directed toward the religious leaders and Pharisees.

In Matthew 23:1–36, Jesus is talking to the crowds and His disciples, but He's really calling out the religious leaders and exposing their hypocrisy. He's telling the people to obey their instructions but do not imitate their behavior.

> So practice and obey whatever they tell you, but don't follow their example. For they don't practice what they teach. They crush people with unbearable religious demands and never lift a finger to ease the burden (Matthew 23:3–4).

Jesus had a problem with the motivation behind what they were doing. I'm not talking about the liturgy of the church. I'm not talking about wearing choir robes in the church choir. I'm not talking about wearing a suit and a tie to church on Sundays. This doesn't indicate whether or not you have a religious spirit. It's the *heart behind* what you're doing that indicates if you have a religious spirit or not. And here's what Jesus is saying in the most scathing way: "Religion doesn't work."

❝ It's the *heart behind* what you're doing that indicates if you have a religious spirit or not.

The Pharisees were some of the most religious people of their day. They desired to put themselves in positions of honor so they would be viewed as *very* important. They wore Tefillin, or prayer boxes, on their arms and above their foreheads in public to win praise of others. During weekday morning prayers throughout the city, the religious leaders would wear small leather cases filled with Scriptures from the Torah by attaching them to a headband or armband. But Jesus saw their hearts and knew much of their motivation for wearing them was for show so everyone would see they were obeying the law.

It's not uncommon for some high priests and rabbis to wear Tefillin today. When Juliette and I went to Jerusalem in 2015, we saw them wearing it throughout the city. It's not only worn to serve as a "sign" and "remembrance" that God brought the children of Israel out of Egypt but also because they are still religious and living by the law of the Old Testament. They're bound to religion. Their motivation for wearing it is out of fear of breaking the law, instead of being motivated by a relationship with Jesus.

I've heard it said we need to keep the Lord on our mind. However, if you have to wear a headband with a box filled with Old Testament Scriptures or a box on your arm with the Torah on the inside to feel like you're close to God, you're doing it all wrong. The majority of people today don't wear Tellefin, but many do something similar for the same reasons: they get Scriptures tattooed on their bodies. Now, if you have Scripture tattooed on you and it means something to you, that's fine. Please hear me—I'm not against tattoos. I actually love them, and I even have one. But if you're doing it so people can see what a great person you are, or if you have to write all your favorite Scriptures on your body so you can feel closer to God, then you're doing it for all the wrong reasons. You're just like the religious leaders Jesus called out in Matthew. You need to ask yourself, "What is the purpose behind it? What is my motivation for doing it?" I'll tell you one thing: Jesus is not up in heaven looking down at you and saying, "Oh sweet! They'll always remember what the Bible says because it's on their wrists and their arms!" No matter what you wear—tattoos or Tellefin or something else—if your heart's motivation is to win the praise of others, then you're doing it for the wrong reasons, and you might have a religious spirit.

Jesus is saying in this passage, "If you're walking around and everything you do is just for show, then your heart is far from God." If you come to church to see if anyone is looking to see if you're there or if you're raising your hands during worship, you have the wrong motive for coming to church. If the reason why you bought a certain outfit is for the compliments people give to you at church, you're showing up for the wrong reason. And here's one that might ruffle some feathers. If you have a certain title or distinction you demand to go by, then you care more about your *verb* than your *noun*. You care more about what you do than who you are.

I tell people all the time to call me Tim, not "Pastor Tim." In fact, I tell everyone who is a resident (member) of our Embassy City Church community to call me Tim, not Pastor Tim. And it's because Tim is my noun—*it's who I am.* Pastor is my verb—*it's what I do.* Therefore, calling me Pastor Tim is redundant. If they already know I'm a pastor, then who exactly are they reminding? I already know I'm a pastor. They already know I'm a pastor. So calling me Tim is just fine.

Think about it like this. If I were an Olympic sprinter like Usain Bolt, and I dominated track and field during three different Olympics and came home with nine gold medals, you wouldn't heretofore refer to me as "Sprinter Tim." Of course not! You wouldn't call me the thing I did; you would call me who I am.

Using someone's name is powerful. We see a clear example of this in Acts 19. Paul is traveling through Asia, ministering to people, preaching about the Kingdom of God, and performing miracles. Hearing about all that Paul was doing, the seven sons of Sceva (a chief priest) became influenced and encouraged by his ministry. They decided to go out and start doing what Paul did, preaching in the name of Paul's God. There was just one problem—they didn't know Paul's God. They had never met Him, and they didn't have a relationship with Him.

These brothers went from town to town, preaching in the name of the Lord Jesus Christ and casting out evil spirits. They were more like exorcists or Jewish magicians who used the name of the Lord as a magic formula to cast out evil spirits. One day they met a demon-possessed man who began to bow-up against them. And they said to the demon, "I command you in the name of Jesus, whom Paul preaches, to come out!" (Acts 19:13). What do you think the demon said back to them? Do you think he said, "Apostles I know, and prophets I know, and evangelists I know, and pastors I know, and teachers I know, but who are you?" Of course, he didn't say that. That's their verb. What he said was, "I know Jesus, and I know Paul, but who are **you**?" (Acts 19:15, emphasis added).

Demons don't care about titles. Don't believe me? Look at what happened next: "Then the man with the evil spirit leaped on them, overpowered them, and attacked them with such violence that they fled from the house, naked and battered" (Acts 19:16). You can call yourself the "apostle prophet evangelist of the second-high pastoral teaching of the second diocese spirit jurisdictional regional bishop of the most-high to the third corner of Tennessee," but if you don't have a relationship with Jesus Christ, you will get beat up! Religion doesn't work. It doesn't hold any power. The only thing that has power is the name of Jesus!

As believers, we have the authority to use the name of Jesus. If we're going to upset the world, we need to forgo religion and move into relationship with Jesus Christ.

> **"** If we're going to upset the world, we need to forgo religion and move into relationship with Jesus Christ.

Only then will we have the power and authority to upset the world.

If you think looking and acting like you're religious is going to bring you into some type of special relationship with God, you have severely disconnected yourself from the Christ who came to redeem the law taught by these religious people. Religion isn't Jesus, and Jesus isn't religion. In fact, when you're acting religious, you don't look or act like Jesus. Why? Because religion doesn't look like Jesus. And that's the reason why Jesus hates religion. It looks nothing like Him.

Have you ever thought about how regular Christ looks? He looks different from the Jesus in the movies. He blended in so well with His disciples that when the religious leaders were looking for Jesus to crucify Him, Judas had to kiss Him on the cheek to show the Roman soldiers and Temple guards who He was. If Judas would have kissed Peter, they might have said, "Okay, take him! He must be Jesus." Jesus wasn't walking around on earth in gleaming white robes while everybody else was wearing subdued hues to make Him look better. Jesus didn't come out with His white robe on and say, "Peter, I need you to change what you're wearing. It's just a little bit too white. They'll get confused with my holiness and your sinful nature, so go put on beige or maybe taupe. I'll even let you wear eggshell; just don't wear gleamy white like me." While it might be funny to think about this happening, the reality is Jesus looked just like the guys around Him. Again, it's not what you have on. It's what's in your heart.

Philippians 2:3 says, "Don't be selfish; don't try to impress others. Be humble, thinking of others as better than yourselves." If I had a definition of the way an upsetter should look, this would be it. It's the very antithesis of a religious spirit. If you keep reading, here's what Paul goes on to say: "Don't look out only for your own interests, but take an interest in others, too. You must have the same attitude that Christ Jesus had" (vv. 4–5).

So what attitude did Christ have? It's the complete opposite of what religion says we should have. Jesus didn't come here to impress the people around Him. Even though He was God, He willingly gave up that right on our behalf and instead came to earth as a human. He was humble and completely unselfish, so much so that He died a criminal's death on the cross so you and I could live. And because of this, God gave Jesus the *name* above all other names—*not* the title above all other titles. We know He is Immanuel, Wonderful Counselor, Mighty God, Everlasting Father, Prince of Peace, and Lord of all. He's El Shaddai, El "all the things," and Jehovah "everything"! We know He's the embodiment of these names, but here's what the Bible says: He was given a *name* that's above *all* other names, and at that *name*—at the name of Jesus—"*every* knee should bow in heaven and on earth and under the earth, and *every* tongue will declare that Jesus Christ is Lord" (Philippians 2:10–11).

Demons are not going to bow because you say, "In the name of the Savior," "In the name of the Crucified," or "In the name of Christ Anointed." Those are titles. Jesus was given a *name*. And that name is above all names. Demons tremble at *His name*. Angels bow in reverence to *His name*, and everyone on earth will too. *His name*, not His title, has power. And because we have a relationship with Him, we have that same power.

The reason Jesus was so angry when He addressed the religious leaders in Matthew 23 is that they cared more about their religion than their relationship with God. When you read this passage, you can assume a little bit of what His tone might have been by the exclamation marks behind certain words, specifically the word *hypocrites*. In fact, He calls them "hypocrites" seven times!

Let's look at another passage in Matthew 23:

What sorrow awaits you teachers of religious law and you Pharisees. Hypocrites! For you shut the door of the Kingdom of Heaven in people's faces. You won't go in yourselves, and you don't let others enter either (vv. 13–14).

What frustrated Jesus so much about the religious teachers was that the instructions they gave placed incredibly harsh restrictions on people who were trying to do their best to live for God. Instead of helping, the confusing customs they practiced kept them in constant bondage. The law alone was enough. If God had just left us with the Ten Commandments, we would have enough work on our hands to obey those. We don't need to add the other 613 commandments the religious leaders were teaching to the list of things we need to do. Yet the religious leaders were holding people accountable to this corrupt teaching.

Any law we try to uphold outside of the context of Jesus Christ's life and teachings will lead to a religious spirit. All the Law of Moses can be completely summed up in Jesus' life. In Mathew 5:17–20, Jesus says,

> Don't misunderstand why I have come. I did not come to abolish the law of Moses or the writings of the prophets. No, **I came to accomplish their purpose**. I tell you the truth, until heaven and earth disappear, not even the smallest detail of God's law will disappear until its purpose is achieved. So if you ignore the least commandment and teach others to do the same, you will be called the least in the Kingdom of Heaven. But anyone who obeys God's laws and teaches them will be called great in the Kingdom of Heaven.
>
> But I warn you—unless your righteousness is better than the righteousness of the teachers of religious law and the Pharisees, you will never enter the Kingdom of Heaven! (emphasis added).

Here's what Jesus is saying to us: "I'm not trying to change your behavior. I'm trying to change your heart, and if I can change your heart, your mind will change too. If I change your mind, it will lead to changed behavior. But we're not going to give all these rules and regulations to try to keep you in place, because it's never worked."

Let's look at the things religious people say to us.

- "If you go to a baseball game, you're going to hell."
- "If you have a beard, you're going to hell."
- "If you have a tattoo, you're going to hell."
- "If you wear a low-cut blouse to church, you're going to hell."
- "Don't watch TV. It's the one-eyed demon, and you'll go to hell!"
- "You better be at church for every Sunday morning service, Sunday evening service, Tuesday night Bible study, Wednesday night main Bible study, and Thursday night prayer meeting. And if you miss *any* of those services, you may not be right with God, which means you're going to hell."

Have you ever experienced this religious spirit? It's the unbearable regulations on top of what the Holy Spirit is convicting us of that cause us to be in perpetual bondage. Now there are things that are just plain sin, but it's not religion that tells us what sin is. It's the Holy Spirit who convicts us of sin. We should live a life that is *worthy* of what Jesus did on the cross. We don't come to church every weekend to get a list of "what not to do." This is one of the things that turns so many people off from church. Do you know what a lot of people are saying about church and why they don't want to come? They're saying, "Oh, it's just a bunch of rules and regulations." They're responding to religion. They're responding to the religious dogma that has so much "extra" on top of living a life for Jesus Christ. That's why Jesus said religion is not appealing to anybody, and it doesn't work.

After I was saved, I was so hungry for the Word and to understand the things of God. My appetite for learning more about God was opened up, and I was devouring *everything* I could get my hands on. But what I learned from my experience with the Bible study leader is that it's important to make sure you're devouring the right food. Sometimes you have to check to make sure what you're putting on your plate to eat is good food. You need to make sure what you're eating is really chicken and not some chicken byproduct. You need to ask questions. Where did it come from? Was it grass-fed or grain-fed? Is it like the chicken some fast food restaurants used to sell—you know, the mix of chicken and other things probably not fit for human consumption? Real, good food will come in and go straight out. But if it's bad food, it will get in you, and it will be hard to come out. It will stay in your system for years. This is why so many people are leaving the Church. They can't get the bad food they've devoured out of their system, and they end up holding a grudge and going on a fast from the truth because the whole time they thought they were eating chicken, they were really eating dog food.

When the leader told me I had to speak in tongues to be saved, what he was really doing was looking at his "to-do list" and telling me I needed another checkmark. That's just religion! It doesn't change my salvation. Once I started asking questions and checking to see if what he was feeding me was good food, I discovered that what he was feeding me was really dog food.

Six months after I got saved, I was baptized in the Holy Spirit. There wasn't a prayer revival, and I didn't have to follow any rules or be in a certain place doing a certain thing. Both of my parents were at work, and I was at home, praying in their room. It was 2:22 a.m., and I was on my knees, just praying and thanking God for things. Then I ran out of stuff to pray for, and boom! This beautiful language started flowing out of my mouth. My mind didn't go blank, my eyes didn't roll in the back of my head, and I wasn't scared. For 20 minutes I prayed in this language. I knew it wasn't gibberish; there was structure and syntax to it. It was beautiful! And I didn't have to use a checklist to make sure I was doing everything the "right" way. I received my prayer language, and it was amazingly easy and fantastic. *No deep, religious experience necessary.*

Here's what I want you to understand: Jesus wants to free us from the religious trappings of the to-do list. There is a discipleship process you need to take as you grow in your relationship with the Lord, but if you've really given your life to Jesus, you will hunger for it and want to dig into it. You won't need pastors and churches holding you to laws that only keep you in bondage.

" Jesus wants to free us from the religious trappings of the to-do list.

As upsetters, we need to be a group of people who have a *desire* to please God as opposed to being *forced* to please God. As I've said in our engaged (new members) class at Embassy City, "If you are a resident of this community, come to church, but don't feel like you have to be here every week." This freaks so many people out. They look at me like I'm crazy and say, "What?!" I tell them, "Go on vacation. You don't have to plan your vacations in between Sundays. That's a religious spirit."

Growing up, I knew so many families who would plan their vacations around church. And if they couldn't be at church, they'd make sure to go to one while they were on vacation. Thoughts such as "We'll leave on Monday, come back on Saturday because we have to be there on Sunday and get counted in the Kingdom" are religious thoughts. I'm not even at the church every Sunday. I'm going on a vacation, so you should too.

If I haven't convinced you yet, let me prove it to you. This may sound familiar. You may even remember hearing it or reading it when you were going through a hard time or needed encouragement. In Matthew 11:28, Jesus says, "Come to Me, all of you who are weary and carry heavy burdens." Jesus is talking to anyone who is bound to religious laws. He says, "Come to Me, because you've been carrying a very heavy burden. If you're trying to adhere to the Mosaic Laws and the 613 *other* laws you've read about, you must be exhausted and tired." If you go a little further, Jesus continues:

> Take My yoke upon you. Let Me teach you, because I am humble and gentle at heart, and you will find rest for your souls. For My yoke is easy to bear, and the burden I give you is light (vv. 29–30).

Here's what Jesus is saying to us: "I know you've been surrounded by all that religious dogma. If you just come straight to Me, you'll immediately feel so light." It may even surprise you how light you feel. You may wonder, *Wait, Jesus! I thought there would be more to it than this. Are you sure this is all I have to do?* And He'll gently say, "Oh child, that's all you need to do. We're done now. Now enjoy life free from all the heaviness."

RELIGION = RULES, BUT JESUS = GRACE

When my wife gave her life to Jesus Christ at the age of nine, she began praying for her father from that day until his last. Her father was an angry man who had hated God his entire life. I don't mean he just disliked God; he *hated* Him. If you listened to a religious program on the radio or watched Christian television in his home, he would go into a rage and begin cussing and throwing things at you. He would even get mad if anyone said the name of God or quoted a Scripture when he was around. So you can imagine how unhappy Juliette and I expected him to be when he found out his daughter decided to marry a preacher.

Before she took me to Jamaica to meet him for the first time, I checked the currency rate for the Jamaican dollar to the American dollar. Then I pulled out a few hundred dollars from my bank account to take with me. When I met her father for the first time, I gave him a "holy handshake" with the money folded in the palm of my hand. He took the money and welcomed me with open arms! Every time I went to visit him from that point on, I took money with me and gave it to him as soon as we arrived.

Scripture says,

A man's gift makes room for him,
and brings him before great men" (Proverbs 18:16 NKJV).

And the New Living Translation puts it like this: "Giving a gift can open doors; it gives access to important people!" I've known many teachers and pastors who have taught that this verse is about spiritual gifts. But this verse is in the Old Testament and has nothing to do with spiritual gifts. It's about a bribe. Think about this: a guy goes to a club and he's told he can't get in, but then he hands a stack of cash to the bouncer and all of a sudden, the red velvet rope is moved, and he goes right in. His gift made room for him. You might be thinking, *Did Tim really just tell me it's okay to bribe someone?* Yes, I did! The truth is the bribe has never been the issue; the motive behind the bribe is the problem.

I continued to give Juliette's dad money every time we came to Jamaica. When he saw me walking up, he'd shout, "Son! It's so good to see my son!" And we would engage in another holy handshake.

Then in 2011, when he was 72 years old, he fell and injured himself and was bound to a wheelchair. Then he was diagnosed with lung cancer, and his health began to decline rapidly. In January 2012, Juliette, her sister, and her mom went to see him. I couldn't go, because I was in Australia, so I recorded a video greeting for him on my iPad. While I was talking to him, I began to share about Christ. I figured it was worth a shot to see if he wanted to give his life to the Lord. I wasn't there in person, so I knew he couldn't punch me in the face. The worst thing he could do was crack the screen on his iPad.

When Juliette showed him the video and it got to the part where I said, "Dad, I've been praying for you. Maybe your heart is open to receiving Jesus Christ," his smile went away. He finished watching the video, and when it was over, he flipped over the iPad and that was it.

On the day Juliette was scheduled to come back home, my father-in-law called and asked her, "When is Tim coming?"

Juliette said, "I don't know, Dad. He can't come now, but he'll come when he gets home from Australia."

That seemed to make him happy. But I still had a packed speaking schedule and couldn't go right away. The next month I was in Dothan, Alabama, when I got a call that his health had severely declined and I needed to get to Jamaica right away.

I flew to Jamaica and got to his house 12 hours before he died. While I was on my way to his room, the nurses stopped me in the hallway. They told me he had been nervous and fidgety for the last few days, and he hadn't been sleeping. This report, along with knowing what an angry man he was, left me feeling a little unsure of what I was about to experience.

As I stepped into his bedroom, I immediately heard the death rattle in his throat. If you've ever been with someone who is near death and heard the sound of their fluids accumulating in their throat and chest, you know this sound. It's unforgettable. His breathing was labored, and his organs were shutting down. He was literally on his deathbed.

I can't help being who I am at all times, even when I'm visiting someone near death, so per my usual self, I shouted, "Dad! I came to see you!"

He lifted his frail body up on the bed and with a gravelly, desperate voice said, "I need you to pray for me!" Then he sank back down onto the bed.

"Dad, that's why I came here," I said.

I sat down next to him on the bed, grabbed his hand, and prayed for him. Suddenly, all the fidgeting they told me he had been doing for the last 48 hours ceased, and he immediately went to sleep. But he was still holding my hand. Trying to be sensitive and let him sleep, I slowly began to ease my hand away. But every time I tried to move, he woke up, clinched my hand, and looked at me with an expression on his face that said, "Uh-uh, don't do that!"

I stayed there, holding his hand and watching him sleep, for 45 minutes. Then I heard the Holy Spirit say, "Get your Bible and read Romans 10:9 to your father-in-law."

I reached over with my free hand and got my Bible off the nightstand. I turned to the passage and said, "Hey Dad, read this" as I put the Bible in front of him.

Dad looked at me and said, "I can't see that."

Then the Holy Spirit said, "*Read* it to him." (I immediately knew I should have listened to Him the first time.)

"Okay, let me read it to you. It says, 'If you confess with your mouth the Lord Jesus and believe in your heart that God has raised Him from the dead, you will be saved.' Daddy, do you believe this?"

He leaned up on the bed and said with as much vigor as he could muster, "I do!"

I said, "Dad, you're saved!"

And he leaned back in the bed and just kept nodding his head in affirmation. My father-in-law, the man who spent his whole life hating God, received Jesus Christ as his personal savior with a nod of affirmation.

Now, religion would tell him that if he didn't say the verse out loud, then he really isn't saved. To take it one step farther, religion says you need to say the sinner's prayer in order to be saved.

"Repeat after me. Dear Lord,"
"Dear Lord,"
"I know that I am a sinner and that I deserve to go to hell."
"I know that I am a sinner and that I deserve to go to hell."
"I believe that Jesus Christ died on the cross for my sins."
"I believe that Jesus Christ died on the cross for my sins."
"I do now receive Him as my Lord and personal Savior."
"I do now receive Him as my Lord and personal Savior."
"I promise to serve you to the best of my ability."
"I promise to serve you to the best of my ability."
"Please save me."
"Please save me."
"In Jesus' name,"
"In Jesus' name,"
"Amen."
"Amen."

What verse in the Bible says *this* is the prayer we need to pray when we receive Christ? There's nothing wrong with this prayer, but when a man is on his deathbed and can hardly talk, you can't tell me I have to hear him verbally go through this back and forth.

" What verse in the Bible says *this* is the prayer we need to pray when we receive Christ?

Just imagine. "Okay, Dad, repeat after me."

"Son, I'm almost dead."

"No, no, you have to get to the end of this prayer, or you're going to hell! We have three more paragraphs left. Come on, Dad. You can do it! You won't get into the Kingdom without saying the sinner's prayer."

This is so ridiculous! It's a religious spirit.

I read him the Scripture, he believed in an affirmation, and 12 hours later, he was in the presence of his Father.

A year later, Juliette and I were at Gateway Church, where I was serving as a pastor at the time, and we were part of their presbytery service. If you've never been to a presbytery service, it's a prophetic service when two or three people (usually elders, pastors, and teachers) who have the gifts of knowledge and prophecy speak encouraging and edifying words into your life. Most of the time, the presbyters are people you've never met, and they don't know anything about you—not even your name.

When it was our turn to receive our prophetic words, one of the presbyters came up to us and asked, "Hey Tim, is your dad here?" I said, "Yes" and pointed to him. Then the second presbyter asked about my mom, and I pointed to her. Then he asked about my mother-in-law, so I pointed to her. Two of the three presbyters had acknowledged three of our four parents. The last presbyter walked straight up to Juliette and said, "Hey Juliette, you know there's been something said about Tim's dad and mom as well as your mom, but last night when I was in prayer the Holy Spirit told me He wanted me to tell you that your father is pleased with you."

God is the God of the living, not the dead, so when He says He is the God of Abraham, Isaac, and Jacob, it's because these guys are *with* Him. He's not talking about dead guys. He's talking about people who are eternally alive with Him. So when the third presbyter said, "Yesterday, I wrote down on this piece of paper that God wanted me to tell you your father is pleased with you," what he was really saying is, "Juliette, your father is in heaven with Jesus!" Eternally, forevermore. Twelve hours before he died, he received Christ in the most non-religious way possible.

When somebody wants to give his or her life to Jesus, you don't have to worry about all the "stuff." You don't have to make sure they've followed a checklist or that they've done things in a particular order. That's not what Jesus did. He didn't tell them to stop doing what they were doing. He received them as they were. He didn't hold them accountable to a list of rules they didn't even know existed. How could they know what they needed to do? They weren't believers yet. They hadn't read the Bible.

My younger brother, Myles, called my dad in the middle of the night while drinking a 40-ounce beer. He was halfway done with his beer when the Holy Spirit convicted him of his sin, and he knew he needed to get saved. My father worked nights at the post office and didn't keep his cell phone with him. Right before my brother called, the Holy Spirit told my dad to go outside and get his cellphone from his car. So he went out to his car, got his cellphone, turned it on, and immediately, it rang.

"Dad, I need to give my life to Jesus. Do I have to wait until Sunday?"

"No, son, you don't have to wait until Sunday," my dad said. "If you confess with your mouth and believe in your heart that Jesus Christ is Lord, you'll be saved."

Myles said, "Oh yeah, I'll say that. Thank you, Dad."

Then he hung up the phone, gave his life to Jesus, and finished his beer. It's hilarious. But it's true. Religion tries to make us think we have to wait until Sunday or we have to be in a church building or we have everything right in our lives. But that's not what the Bible says. The Bible says Jesus will never reject those who come to Him (John 6:37). It doesn't say we have to have everything together. We don't have to be perfect. We just have to come to Him, right where we are. Religion would make us think we have to follow certain rules or rituals before we come to Him. This is just another reason why Jesus hates religion.

Upsetters aren't religious, because Jesus isn't religious. You were counted in the Kingdom when you gave your life to Jesus, so don't be religious. Instead, let the relational love of Jesus Christ make you commit your life to Him each and every day. If you want to upset the world, get rid of religion and get in relationship with Jesus.

" Upsetters aren't religious, because Jesus isn't religious.

CHAPTER 6
UPSETTERS DO GOOD

Holy Spirit, help me do good so I can upset people. Amen.

Have you ever set out to do something good for someone else, and it didn't turn out quite as you expected? This happened to me a couple of years ago. Joshua Brown with Daystar Television Network called me and said, "Hey, Tim, we want to bless some people, so we're going to load up a couple of trucks with some supplies for homeless people and drive to downtown Dallas and give everything away. Are you in?"

"Absolutely! Let's do it!"

Several weeks later, I met Joshua and some of the other guys from Daystar a few days before Thanksgiving. Before I got there, they had packed two big SUVs to the brim with anything and everything a homeless person might need. We had tents and thermal blankets. We had gift cards to give them so they could buy things they needed or go to a restaurant and eat a warm meal. And we had tons of backpacks. These weren't empty backpacks. They were filled with toothbrushes, toothpaste, thermal underwear, long johns, long sleeve shirts, gloves, scarves, hats, beanies ... all the necessities one might need.

This day had been chosen weeks before, and we had no idea that it would be the third coldest day of the year. With the extremely cold temperatures, we were ready to get going so we could get these much-needed supplies to people as soon as possible. So we jumped into the SUVs with all of our gifts and supplies and headed to downtown Dallas. But there was one problem. When we got there, we couldn't find anyone to help! There wasn't a homeless person to be found on the streets of Dallas that day. Most of the time, this would've been a good thing because it would have meant that more people were finding jobs and getting off the streets. However, we knew something had to be going on. There was no way they could *all* be gone!

We started driving through the areas in the city where most of the homeless people hang out, but the streets were empty.

We looked under bridges and in places we knew were heavily populated with homeless people, but we couldn't find anyone. We refused to give up and kept driving all over the city of Dallas. Still, no one. We hunted for people to bless for *five hours*.

If you haven't been to downtown Dallas before, let me fill you in on something: you don't need to *try* to find homeless people. They are not hard to find. You can usually find them under overpasses or panhandling at most major intersections. But here's the crazy part. Because it was so cold and someone had frozen to death on the streets the night before, all the homeless people had been corralled by the police and taken off the streets. They put as many people as possible in shelters and then put the others in jail just to get them off the streets and keep them in a warm place. That's why we couldn't find them!

We started off with the intentionality to do good, but things didn't go according to our plan. You see, we wanted to find some people to bless, so we set aside two hours (11 a.m. to 1 p.m.) on this specific day to go out and do some good. But we didn't find anybody we could bless during those two hours. Sometimes we like to do good on our own terms and when it's convenient for us. We say things like, "Well, I'm done. I tried to do good, but it's cold. Let's just take the backpacks and all these supplies back home and come out another day." But if we're going to upset the world, we can't let small obstacles get in our way. We can't let our plans get in the way of God's plans. So we said, "We're not leaving until we find some people we can bless!"

" We can't let our plans get in the way of God's plans.

After driving around for several hours, we prayed, "Holy Spirit, will You please lead us to some people we can bless?" It was right after that prayer that we turned and wound up under an overpass, and there were two homeless men on sitting on a pile of trash right next to their shopping carts filled with all their belongings. We could tell they were cold, and we were so excited to be able to give them some things to help them stay warm.

We jumped out of the SUVs and walked over to them. I got down on my knees and hugged one of the guys and said, "Hey man, how are you?"

He said he was fine, but he and his friend looked over at the cameras and then back at us, and we could tell they were suspicious about why we were there. Trying to ease their concerns, I said, "Hey, if you guys don't mind, we're just filming our time out here. We're here to be a blessing to you, and we would like to know what your needs are."

They immediately put their guards down and began to open up to us. The man I talked with had more wisdom to give me than I had to give him. I asked him how long he had been on the streets, and he said it was somewhere between nine and eleven years.

"How have you survived on the streets for *nine* years?" I asked.

"I just take it one day at a time," he said.

This hit me hard. It's not what you usually hear from a person who is down on their luck. Typically, you hear, "Oh, it's been rough. I lost my job, and I lost my family. I don't have anything." Or they whine and complain. But his perspective was *totally* different. He was in survival mode, and in order to survive, he had to take it one day at a time. There's a verse in the Bible that summarizes this perspective beautifully: "So don't worry about tomorrow, for tomorrow will bring its own worries. Today's trouble is enough for today" (Matthew 6:34). This homeless man made me look through the lens of my bougie, suburban perspective and think, *Why am I worrying about anything? Why am I letting my bills drive me crazy? Why am I allowing that situation at work to ruin my day?* The realization that this guy had survived nine years on the street by living out this principle reminded me that this is how we all need to be leading our lives. One day at a time. No one is promised tomorrow. We need to do good *today*.

We talked for a little while longer, and before we left, I asked him if I could pray for him. He was so open and receptive to me praying for him. It was like he had just been waiting for me to ask. Then we gave he and his friend some supplies along with some gift cards to Denny's and some cash. I hugged him, and then we set out to find some more people.

When you're doing good, you have to do as the Holy Spirit leads. You can't put rules and regulations on your gifts. Many people will say not to give a homeless person cash. "Oh, you know what he'll do with it! He won't buy food; he'll just go buy alcohol!" Or "She's going to waste all that money buying drugs." Stop it. Just give them the money. You're there to do good, and hopefully you're being led by the Holy Spirit. It's not your responsibility to tell them what they can and can't do with the provision you're giving them. Unless you're bringing them to your house or you have a long-term solution to get them off the streets, you can't govern them and tell them what they can and can't do with the money. If you're giving them a twenty-dollar bill, you can't worry about how they're going to use it. If you don't feel comfortable giving money, then don't give it. But if you're going to give it, don't give it with stipulations. Don't tell them they have to buy food with it. Just give it to them!

As we pulled away, we felt the Holy Spirit leading us to go back to an area where a lot of homeless people usually hang out, even though no one was there earlier in the day. When we went back, we saw people pouring out into the streets by the dozens! The shelters had just kicked them all out from the previous night's corralling. So what did we do? We pulled into the parking lot, popped open the back of the SUVs, and shouted, "Backpacks! Tents!"

Within four minutes, the backpacks were gone, the tents were gone ... *everything* in both SUVs was gone. While it was incredible to be doing good and blessing people with things they desperately needed, the fact everything we had was gone within minutes wasn't lost on us. That was the saddest part. We were heartbroken that everything went so quickly. These people desperately needed these things, and we only wished we'd brought more because there were still countless people who didn't get anything.

They would walk up to us and ask, "Hey, do you have another tent?" Sadly, we'd have to say, "Man, I'm so sorry. We don't." We were brokenhearted that we didn't have anything left to give, but their disposition was incredible! All of them responded pretty much the same way: "That's okay. Thanks for coming down here anyway." It blew us away!

Some of them didn't want to be filmed on camera, and we were fine with that. We didn't go downtown for a photo op. We weren't there solely to get it on film. We really wanted to do good and thought it would be a great story for the Daystar audience. If the homeless people didn't want to be on camera, we'd tell them, "You don't have to be on camera, but please take a backpack. We want you to have this." And then I'd give them a hug. And they were so grateful!

We set out to upset some people in Dallas by doing good. But you know what? It turns out they upset us just as much. The unintended incredible effect of being a blessing to somebody is how much it blesses us in return. Whether it's a homeless person telling me, "One day at a time" or Jesus telling us, "Don't worry about tomorrow."

FOLLOWING THE LEADER

The reason we should do good is that it upsets the world. And Jesus is the One who shows us how to do good. If you want to know the whole formula for upsetting the world, it's right here in Acts 10:38: "And you know that God anointed Jesus of Nazareth with the Holy Spirit and with power. Then Jesus went around **doing good** and healing all who were oppressed by the devil, for God was with him" (emphasis added). All too often when people read this verse, they skip over the part about Jesus doing good, and they focus on Jesus healing the people who were demon-possessed. They get all worked up and start yelling, "The devil is alive! Let's go get the oil and cast out those demons!" Yes, as believers, this is part of what we do. We believe there's a demonic spiritual realm, and God's given us all authority over it. We don't have to shout and scream at the demons, though. We don't need antics. We can just take authority and cast them out. We stand firm in the authority we have in Jesus Christ, not how loud our voice can get as we cast them out. But there's something else we need to do at the same time. There's a sequence we need to follow in this verse. Did you see what Jesus did before He healed people who were demon-possessed? He went around *doing good*. **You want to know how to upset the world?** *Do good.* We live in a *very* cynical world. Do you know what can make a demon run faster than pouring out some oil? Being nice. You want to upset someone? Be nice and do something good for them.

> **"** You want to know how to upset the world?
> *Do good.*

No matter what denomination you might have been raised in or what theological persuasion you might lean toward, it always seems as though people are split two ways. There are people who love doing good works for Jesus, and then there are people who just want the power of Jesus to do miracles, cast out demons, and heal those who are oppressed. Here's what I'm saying: *do both*. I just want to make it really, really simple. It's not "either-or"; it's "both-and." Jesus went around doing good *and* healing all those who were oppressed by the devil.

Did you know you have the authority to heal those who are oppressed by demons? You received that authority when you came into a relationship with Jesus. It's not something you have to work up to or pray for or anything you can do on your own. The moment you became a citizen of heaven, you gained all the rights of those who come from that country. One of those rights is to be empowered by the Holy Spirit to take authority over spiritual wickedness in high places—the principalities in this world—but *not* at the expense of doing good. We shouldn't be so focused on this that we forget to do good things.

This is what I love about Jesus. He loved to do good. And He showed us how much He liked to do good when He performed His first miracle at a wedding (see John 2:1–12). His mom tells Him they've run out of wine at the reception, and Jesus says, "No one has to go anywhere. No need to run to the grocery store. I got this!" His mother then tells the servants to do whatever her Son says. Jesus tells them to fill up the six huge water pots with water. These weren't just any water pots. They were the ones used for washing the hands and feet of the people who came to the wedding. Once they were all filled, Jesus told them to dip out some wine and take it to the master of ceremonies. The servants did as He said and took a glass of wine to the headmaster who exclaimed, "You saved the best for last!"

It's crazy if you really think about it! They've been waiting on Jesus to come to this world for 4,000 years. He could have been anywhere, doing anything, yet He chose to start His earthly ministry at a wedding. And out of all the miracles He could have started with to proclaim His messianic arrival, He chose to fill dirty water pots with water and turn it into the best-tasting wine! This was His first miracle *ever*! It wasn't blind eyes being opened, a lame hand stretching out, a person who couldn't walk standing up, a dead body coming back to life. No. His first miracle was turning water into wine. Why? Because He's a good guy who likes to do good. He's just nice. John 2:11 says, "This miraculous sign at Cana in Galilee was the first time Jesus revealed his glory. And his disciples believed in him." If we want people to believe what we have to say, we need to do good because they need to see Jesus in us.

And here's the thing: Jesus never stopped doing good. After He kicked off His earthly ministry at the wedding, He traveled around preaching, and everywhere He went crowds gathered. On one particular day while He was preaching, a large crowd amassed, and He was moved with compassion when He saw how hungry they were. And this wasn't a small crowd. There were 5,000 men sitting on the hill that day, and this didn't include any women or children who may have been with them. Altogether, there could have potentially been 12,000 to 18,000 people out there listening to Jesus' message (Matthew 14:13–21). To them, being there and hearing Him teach was more important than eating, but He saw how hungry they were, so He decided to feed them and sent His disciples out to find food.

Can you imagine how you'd feel if you were one of the disciples? You want to please Jesus and do as He says, but what He's asked of you is an impossible task. There is no way humanly possible to feed this many people. It's miles to the nearest store, and there aren't any restaurants nearby. None of these disciples had any restaurant management experience or knew how to feed huge parties. They didn't know what they were going to do! They looked at each other and said, "What if we find all the people who brought their lunches and put them together? Maybe that will be enough to feed this crowd." And then Andrew, one of Jesus' disciples, found a boy with a sack lunch. He rummaged around the bag and found two fish and five loaves of bread. He rushed over to Jesus and said, "I found some fish and bread!"

Jesus turned to His disciples and said, "Get all the people to sit down in groups of fifty." Then He blessed the bread, broke it, and started handing it out. And a miracle happened. The baskets stayed full of bread and fish until everyone had eaten. Not just the first ten people who got in line early for this conference at the lake. It wasn't just for the people who preregistered and got their meal tickets ahead of time. He fed *everybody*. Why?

Because He likes to do good. Because He's kind. Because He's a nice guy.

It was nice of Jesus when He saw Zacchaeus, the chief tax collector, in a tree and told him, "Hey, come down! I'm coming to your house for dinner." That was just nice of the Messiah who, in the midst of everything He had to do before going to the cross, said, "I'm going to have dinner at Zacchaeus's house because I feel like it." It doesn't get much nicer than that!

When a religious man named Nicodemus asked Jesus questions about who He was, Jesus was nice enough to hang out with the guy late at night and answer his questions. Why? Because He's a nice guy.

When you're genuinely nice and do good things, you're being like Jesus, and like Him, you're going to upset people. The apostle Paul told believers,

> So let's not get tired of doing what is good. At just the right time we will reap a harvest of blessing if we don't give up. Therefore, whenever we have the opportunity, we should do

good to everyone—especially to those in the family of faith (Galatians 6:9–10).

When I talk to people about this, I often hear excuses about why they can't be nice. "Well, it's not my personality to go out and do good." "I'm not really a people-person." (We already talked about that one. Yes, you are!) I've even heard people say they're standoffish when it comes to being around people they don't know. Maybe you were a standoffish person *before* you met Jesus, but now you're reborn, and, thanks to the Holy Spirit, you're no longer that person!

As a believer, you can't make boundary lines of where Jesus can and cannot have access to your life. He has to be Lord of your *whole* life. The enemy is looking for the markers you make to see where you have drawn the line of not submitting to Christ's lordship. That's the place in your life where he's going to fight you the most because you've told him where your boundary is. He will put all launch coordinates on that one spot. Wherever you've drawn the line, he's going to create one for you to cross so you can be in his territory.

IT'S WHO WE ARE

Upsetters do good *all the time*. This should be our lifestyle and how we go about our everyday lives. Romans 2:7 says, "He will give eternal life to those who keep on doing good, seeking after the glory and honor and immortality that God offers." You know how you can start? Just do good stuff. Be kind. Be thoughtful. Do good things for people. Simply being nice to someone can have a profound effect on their life. It could be as powerful as raising someone from the dead. Because if you upset them, you are literally saving them from death. It's exactly what Jesus did. He traveled around doing good everywhere he went.

Things won't always go the way you plan. We didn't plan to drive to Dallas and not find one single person we could bless. It's important for us to remember what Proverbs 16:9 says:

> We can make our plans,
>   but the Lord determines our steps."

It's not up to us to decide who wants to be upset or who doesn't. It's just our assignment to upset. You can do good stuff to disrupt people in a very practical way that makes them think to themselves, "I have no idea what's going on here, but I like it!" If we're going to upset the world, we have to do good deeds.

> **" It's not up to us to decide who wants to be upset or who doesn't. It's just our assignment to upset.**

Now, here's why I named this book *Upset the World* and not *Upset the City*, *Upset Your House*, or *Upset Your Block*. It's *Upset the World* because we *all* have a world. You have your home life world, you have your work world, and you have your fun, play world. Whatever world you're in, go upset it in the name of Jesus Christ. And as you're doing good, you may also do one of those really awesome things like pray for someone to be healed of cancer, and they are healed. Or pray for someone to be delivered from an evil spirit, and they receive freedom. But let me tell you what you'll be doing every day if you don't do any of the "big stuff" that gets celebrated in church—you'll be doing good. You'll be turning people's lives upside down, changing them forever. Every day we should be asking God, "Will you put me in a position to do good today? Will you show me someone I can be nice to and do good to today?" If we all commit to doing good, we *will* upset the world.

CHAPTER 7
UPSETTERS LOVE LIFE

Holy Spirit, give me a joy that will upset the world. Amen.

I've always been a very expressive and joyful person. My mom would tell you I've been that way from the time I was born. I was a joyful, happy baby, and it's who I am to this day. It's how God created me. But there was a time in my life when that joy got pushed so far down that I had to fake being happy.

When I was eight years old, I was molested by a neighbor who lived across the street from me. And it wasn't a one-time act. It happened over and over again for six or seven months, and it was traumatic. I did everything I could to manufacture an outwardly expressive and happy persona so no one would know what was going on, because I was terrified for my parents to find out. I didn't want them to think anything had changed, but deep down, I was carrying this dark secret, and it was tearing me up inside. The first time it happened, I remember thinking, "I can't tell my dad what just happened because he will kill that man."

There are no eight-year-olds who should be having thoughts like that. My son Noah turned eight years old last October. I don't fear for him, and I wasn't afraid for my other son, Nathan, when he was younger. But it doesn't stop me from remembering the things I thought about when I was his age. Right now, all Noah cares about is Fortnite, iPhones, and Real Steal Box. I should have been thinking about He-Man, Big Wheels, and Transformers. For me to think about my dad killing a man was scary, and I convinced myself that I had to keep what happened to me a secret. Why? I didn't want my dad to go to prison for murder.

This led to the first time I consciously told a lie. I can remember it like it was yesterday. I came home from school, and my mom asked me, "How was your day?" And I said, "Fine." I knew I was lying. It wasn't like I got caught with my hand in the cookie jar and said I didn't take any. I was scared to death. The real answer to her question was, "I can't tell you the truth because it's too horrific." So I pushed it down and tried to act like everything was okay and nothing had changed.

I forced myself to be happy. I was still an outwardly expressive person, but I was putting on a show so no one would see the truth. I began to play a role as the "happy and funny boy," so people wouldn't ask me what was wrong. I became the class clown and did everything I could to deflect and redirect people so they wouldn't see the truth. Not only did my personality change, but I couldn't focus at school and had trouble keeping my grades up. They were atrocious. When I think back to my fifth and sixth grade years, all I see and feel is darkness. *It's just so dark.*

Then when I was 12 years old, I was exposed to pornography. For me, looking at pornography made me feel the same way a hit of cocaine makes a drug addict feel or the way taking a drink feels for an alcoholic. It was exhilarating, and it became my drug. I didn't know what this feeling was, but I wanted more of it. Flash forward, and I'm 19 years old and a full-blown porn addict. It's ruling my life. This isn't a casual thing I'm doing. I can't control my impulses. I knew in my heart what I was doing was wrong, but like any addiction, it had a tight hold on me. I couldn't stop even though I wanted to. I remember thinking one day, *If I got caught by my mom, I'd probably stop, because I'd be so embarrassed. I'd be mortified if she caught me looking at pornography. It would probably be enough to shake me out of this.*

Wouldn't you know, within a few weeks of having that thought, I got caught by my mom. It was 2 a.m., and I was watching porn on our big screen television in the back of the house. I didn't hear her walking down the hall, and she walked right in on me and saw it all. It was *horrible*! It was so bad.

I was mortified. Embarrassed. Sick. Devastated. She didn't say a word, though. She just turned around and went right to her room, got on her knees, and started praying.

I was distraught. I jumped out of the chair and grabbed the tape out of the VCR. As I walked down the hall, I realized I had a choice. I could make a right turn to go to my parents' room and finally face the truth. Or I could make a left turn and go to my room and pretend nothing ever happened. Here were my exact thoughts: *If I go to my room, I could stay in there for three or four days and hope this whole thing just goes away. It's awkward, and she'll probably tell Dad, and he'll yell and be mad. But everything will be fine by Friday. I'll wait out any drama that may happen on Monday, Tuesday, Wednesday, and Thursday, and everything will be fine by Friday. But if I make a right turn, and I go into their room, I will have to tell my momma why porn is an issue.* I knew why it had a grip on me, and it terrified me to tell her.

Even though I wasn't a Christian at the time, it was as though the Holy Spirit gave me the power to make the choice to turn right and go into their room. As I opened their door, I could see my mom on her knees praying, her face wet with tears from crying.

I looked at her and said, "Mom, I don't want you to think I'm nasty, and I don't want you to think I'm dirty, but I got molested when I eight." I was 19 years old, but at that moment it was as though the eight-year-old little boy walked into his mommy's room and finally told her what happened.

She started crying harder, and then we woke up Myles. When I was 15 and he was 14, I had found out that the same neighbor molested him. Once we figured out that it had happened to both of us, we decided to take all our pent-up anger, shame, and guilt and do something about it. The man who did this to us had gone to prison for another offense, but he was going to be released soon. And when he got out, we were going to kill him. The day they were setting up for his "welcome home from prison" party, we knew what we had to do. We went into our mom's kitchen and got the sharpest knives we could find and stuck them in the back pockets of our jeans. This wasn't a joke. We weren't playing or threatening him. We were going to kill him. Our plan was to walk right up to him at his welcome home party and stab him to death.

We headed over to the party, and as we were walking over, we saw him in the yard. So we called him out into the street between our two houses. He came up to us and was excited to see us. He gave us the biggest hugs and the biggest greeting: "It's so good to see you guys! Wow, you guys have grown!" We looked into his eyes, and he had no clue what he'd done. It was almost like it never happened. I looked over at Myles, and he looked back at me, and we were both wondering what we were going to do. (Myles was on the phone. He always followed my lead, and I knew I had to be the initiator.) We decided to call it off and went back into the house.

We tell our mom this story, and now she's crying harder. She calls my dad at the post office and tells him he needs to come home. He gets home around four o'clock in the morning, and we tell him our stories. I share my story first, then Myles shares his story. But the next thing that happened took us totally by surprise. My mom told us she was sexually abused by her babysitters when she was six years old. And then my dad shared that he gotten molested by a comic book store owner when he was five years old. In one night, all the family secrets were out. It was over.

I've never been drunk, and I've never done drugs, but pornography had a hold of me, and it was like a boulder over my heart. As we all shared that night, the bondage broke. I wasn't completely free of the addiction, but a light was put on it, and the frequency of the occurrences lessened because I was finally able to talk about it. Pornography is a very isolating addiction. There's a reason you're in isolation when you do it; it's because you don't have words. All addictions are because you don't have words. Whatever doesn't come up and out of your mouth with words will come up and out of your body with actions. Because if you don't have a word to put to it, your body is going to manifest in some other way.

Six months later, I gave my life to Christ, and that's when the boulder was lifted and my new life began. That was the *only* thing that was holding me back. In full disclosure, I have had over a decade of counseling because I wasn't satisfied with stopping the action. I wanted to get to the root. That's the investigator in me. I want to know the cause. Then I had to deal with the question, "What made me get to the point where I wanted to murder someone?" That took about another decade of counseling.

THE JOY OF THE LORD

You may be thinking, *Why is Tim sharing this story in a chapter he titled "Upsetters Love Life"?* It's because the story I just shared with you could have *completely* ended my love for life. But it didn't. And if you have a similar story, it doesn't have to end yours either.

So many people allow the negative circumstances of their past to write negativity for every day of their present and future. I've known too many believers who are walking around with a victim mentality. "I got molested, and I still struggle with porn." Or "I had a hard childhood, so I get drunk to ease the pain." I'm not trying to undermine what you went through. Pain is pain. You were hurt. But when are you going to get over it? I knew this could not be the narrative of my entire life, and it shouldn't be yours either.

Jesus came so we could be set free. The apostle Paul told the believers in Rome,

> We know that our old sinful selves were crucified with Christ so that sin might lose its power in our lives. We are no longer slaves to sin. For when we died with Christ we were set free from the power of sin (Romans 6:6–7).

" Jesus wants to bring healing and freedom to every area of your life that is stealing your joy.

When I got saved and started preaching, the thing that was fresh on my mind was freedom from this bondage—the tormenting I experienced as a child that led to the porn addiction. In the beginning, I preached a lot on freedom, but the message of Jesus Christ is a much better gospel than me preaching my testimony. I don't want to be known as the "porn guy who got redeemed." I don't want people to say, "Here comes Tim with his one message. You already know what it is. He was delivered from porn!" I'm going to preach the gospel because the gospel is *amazing,* and everybody fits into it. If I only preached about a porn addiction, not everybody fits in it. Not everyone struggles with addiction. People would say, "That's not my issue, but God bless you, you pervert."

Upsetters have to love life in spite of the negative stuff that happens to them. You have to find where the joy is and ride it out. And where is the joy? It's found in the Lord. The Bible says, "Don't be dejected and sad, for the joy of the Lord is your strength!" (Nehemiah 8:10).

I can tell you with certainty that before I gave my life to Jesus Christ, what I thought I loved about my life, I really didn't. I loved some parts of it. I loved some highlights of it, but I wasn't in love with my *entire* life. When I gave my life to Jesus and started following His example, I started to *love* the life I was living because I had a blueprint of how to *really* live it. And you have this same blueprint. I love what Ephesians 5:2 says: "Live a life filled with love, following the example of Christ. He loved us and offered himself as a sacrifice for us, a pleasing aroma to God." So how can you love life? I'll tell you how. Live a life following the example of Christ, and you will love the life you live. This simple, yet profound truth, changed everything for me! So when I tell you, "Love life! Upsetters, *love* life! You should be zestfully enthusiastic about life!" what I'm really saying is if you follow the example of Jesus Christ, you will love the life you live.

I'm not living under a rock. I know not everyone reading this book loves their lives. And to be honest, I initially struggled with writing this chapter. Not because I was embarrassed or ashamed of my past. It's because if there's anything I loathe as it relates to communicating the gospel message, it's for anything I say to be motivational solely for the sake of being motivational. Someone else might tell you, "Hey, just ignore everything going on around you and think happy thoughts!" Let's be real, though. That line of thinking is ridiculous. True motivation must be empowered by the Holy Spirit, or else it's just a pep talk, and you can get that anywhere. But when I thought about loving life, it just seemed to keep coming up—*upsetters love life!* I kept trying to avoid writing it because I didn't want it to come across as frivolous or hyper motivational. I didn't want you to read this and hear my uber-excited speaker voice saying, "Come on! Just love life! Go out there and get it. Love your life with a passion! Pursue it with abandon!" I finally relented and said, "Holy Spirit, help me with this chapter on why upsetters need to love life." And of course, He said, "Okay, I will, because it's important!"

If we're going to live our lives as upsetters, it means we're going to love Jesus, love people, be spirit-filled, not be religious, do good, and *love life*. You—yes, *you*—can love life. Remember, the joy of the Lord is your strength. Joy that comes from the Lord is what lasts. The joy of the Lord doesn't come from you looking in the mirror and saying, "I'm just going to be happy until I am happy." "If I think positive thoughts, positive things will happen." "If I have positive energy, it all be okay." Um, no. That does not work. That line of thinking is motivational and doesn't last. You need to be filled with the joy of the Lord. It's the only thing that works, and it's the only way you'll truly love life.

There have been some incredibly dark moments in my life. I don't love those dark moments, but I still love my life. I love my life because it's been completely upset by Jesus Christ. He completely overturned *everything* I thought about life and gave me a proper perspective on it. It's because of Him that I can honestly say I really do love my life.

Are there some bad things that happened to me? Absolutely. I'm not superman. I don't wake up every morning and say, "This is the best day ever! Everything is awesome!" Some days are good. Some days are bad. And some days are really bad.

One of the darkest days of my life was when I lost my brother. Myles had been my best friend for practically my whole life. When he was 27 years old, he was driving, and an 18-wheeler pulled out in front of him. Myles thought he had timed the turn right and had enough time to get past the truck, but what he didn't know was the truck had a second full trailer. It caught his car, and he died instantly. He never saw it coming.

Even though that day was dark, I still had the joy of the Lord. It truly was my strength. We can hold on to the promise that says,

> Weeping may last through the night,
> but joy comes with the morning (Psalm 30:5).

A trait of being a believer is being joyful. We have the joy of the Lord. And it's something that upsets others. Our love of life and joy in the Lord will draw people to Him and upset their lives in the best possible way.

David said it best when he cried out to God and asked,

> What will you gain if I die,
>   if I sink into the grave?
> Can my dust praise you?
>   Can it tell of your faithfulness? (Psalm 30:9)

If we're not out there telling people about Jesus' love, what good is our life? How will it help anyone? How can we build His Kingdom if we don't share about His faithfulness? We're not going to upset the world if we look and feel miserable. We won't attract people to Jesus if we're not *joyfully* loving our lives. I'm not saying we need to walk around with a smile on our face singing "la la la-la la la" all the time. But what I am saying is we need to have the joy of the Lord, and we need to love life.

" How can we build His Kingdom if we don't share about His faithfulness?

We know upsetters need to be filled with the Holy Spirit, but do you know what comes with being filled with the Holy

Spirit? Joy! "So the Lord's message spread throughout that region. And the believers were filled with joy and with the Holy Spirit." (Acts 13:49, 52) As we're continuously filled with the Holy Spirit, we're also continuously filled with joy. And we need to share this joy with others.

We need to bring people to the Lord by upsetting them with our joy and love for life. You may remember this song from when you were a child: "I've Got the Joy, Joy, Joy, Joy." It talks about having the joy of the Lord deep down in your heart. When you're filled with the joy of the Lord, it will permeate every ounce of your being. You can't keep it to yourself even if you want to. It's joy that will upset people and make them want to have a relationship with Jesus.

As upsetters, we can't be silent. Nothing can hold us back from sharing the joy of the Lord. It's a joy that's contagious. Even when we have bad days. Even when times are hard. Even when you're molested. Even when your brother dies. Even when (fill in the blank). The joy of the Lord will fill you. It will come, and you will be filled with love for life. Psalm 30:11–12 says,

> You have turned my mourning into joyful dancing.
>> You have taken away my clothes of mourning and clothed me with joy,
> that I might sing praises to you and not be silent.
>> O Lord my God, I will give you thanks forever!"

Want to love your life? Follow the example of Jesus, and you will love the life you're in *right now*. You may be thinking, *But Tim, you don't know my past and where I came from.* I don't have to. Find Jesus, follow His example, and then you will love the life you're in. Let me tell you something: Jesus can redeem *any* life. It doesn't matter that at the age of 8 years old I had been molested or at the age of 12 I was exposed to pornography or by the time I was 19 I was a full-blown porn addict or that my brother died when I was 29. The most upsetting thing that ever happened to me was not the molestation, it wasn't the addiction, and it wasn't my brother's death. It was the overwhelming love of Jesus Christ that turned my life upside down. He did it for me, and He can do it for you too.

" Jesus can redeem *any* life.

CHAPTER 8
UPSETTERS DISTURB THE PIECE

Holy Spirit, help me disturb the piece
so I can upset people. Amen.

B y now you know we've been called and commissioned to upset the world. But now it's time to talk about how we're also called and commissioned to disturb the piece. Yes, you read that correctly. I'm not talking about disturbing the peace by rioting, picketing, or rallying. I'm talking about disturbing the piece of people's lives that's not aligned with God's will, His ways, and His decrees. As ambassadors of Christ, we've been commissioned to upset others by disturbing the piece of them that's not in harmony with Jesus Christ. If we're going to upset the world, it means we're going to interfere with and disarrange the piece in people's lives that's not in alignment with the Word of God.

Think about the times in your life when you've encountered God and have been in His presence, and He disturbed your piece. Maybe He showed up and disturbed your paradigm of thought. Maybe you had a deeply held belief or habit you'd been holding onto for a long time, and all of the sudden He came and disturbed that piece of your life to the point that what was neatly arranged in your mind about how you felt about something was totally rearranged, unharmonized, and turned upside down so you could see it from heaven's perspective. This is how Jesus disturbs our piece.

We see it all throughout the Bible but particularly in the Gospels. Jesus comes into people's lives, and suddenly, everything is turned upside down. They came to Him to get healing for themselves or a sick loved one, to raise someone from the dead, and to fix problems in their lives. People come to Jesus all the time because something is out of alignment, and they want it to be realigned. But what I want you to grasp and understand are the times Jesus chooses to come into our lives and disturb the piece by addressing situations, thoughts, habits, and addictions. When He addresses the sin in our lives, He completely upsets us.

This isn't anything new. Jesus has always liked to disturb the piece. He's been doing it since the beginning of time. But I want us to look at four instances from Jesus's time on earth when He *purposely* and *strategically* addressed the situation in someone's life, and He's the One who instigated it. Not only did Jesus initiate contact, but He also strategically picked the place, the person, and the piece of their lives He wanted to address.

This is going to be good, so get ready!

THE WOMAN

Our first story begins in Judea. Jesus has been spending time teaching and sharing with people, and many of them are getting baptized. The Pharisees hear stories that Jesus "was baptizing and making more disciples than John (though Jesus himself didn't baptize them—his disciples did)." To keep the peace, Jesus decides to leave Judea and return to Galilee, but "He had to go through Samaria on the way" (John 4:1–3).

It's interesting that the Bible says, "He *had* to go through Samaria on the way" because He didn't *have* to go through Samaria. He's Jesus. He can go wherever He wants. And even though Samaria *is* most the direct route from Judea to Galilee, most Jews would have taken the long way around to avoid any contact with the Samaritans. As a Jewish man, Jesus knows the Jewish people have had contention with the Samaritan people for thousands of years, and as we learned in chapter three, most Jews never wanted to come in close proximity to them. Jesus strategically picks the place to come into contact with a Samaritan person so He can disturb her piece.

When He arrives in Samaria, Jesus is tired and worn out from His journey, so He sits down beside Jacob's well to rest. It is lunchtime, so His disciples leave Him to go buy some food.

He is alone when He sees a woman come to the well to draw water, and He says to her, "Please give me a drink" (John 4:7).

Immediately upon arrival in Samaria, Jesus picks the person whose piece He wants to disturb. We know this for two reasons. First, not only was it customary for Jewish people to avoid Samaritans, but they also *never* shared dishes or drinking vessels with them. So not only does He strategically choose this place—Samaria—but He also intentionally chooses this woman when He asks her for a drink. Merely opening his mouth to talk to her made it a divine appointment. (And believe me, Jesus is not going to talk to you unless He really has something to say.)

The Bible gives us another clue as to why Jesus was compelled to go to Samaria at this time to find this woman. The normal routine for women was to go to the well in the morning to draw the water and take it back to their homes for the day. If Jesus was just coming to find any woman to talk to, he would have come in the morning. But He chose to come at noon. The fact that this woman came around noon lets us know she didn't want to be there with the other women. She had been married five times and was filled with guilt and shame. And when Jesus starts a conversation with her, she has no idea she is about to have her piece disturbed. Jesus knows, though.

So they start up a conversation about getting water. She's surprised He's even talking to her and reminds Him that Jews aren't supposed to have anything to do with Samaritans. Jesus tells her that if she had any idea whom she was talking to that she'd ask Him for water and would never be thirsty again. She argues with Him and tells Him there's no way He can give her water. He doesn't even have a bucket or a rope. How could He give her water, let alone water that's better than the water in this well? The very well Jacob and his family used and now most every Samaritan uses.

Then Jesus tells her that if she drinks the water He has to offer, she'll never be thirsty again. Liking the sound of this, she begs Him to give her the water. I imagine her response to Him sounding like this: "Oh, Jesus! If you could come install this well full of water at my house, that would be great! I'll never be thirsty again, and I won't have to keep coming out here to get water. You may not know this, but there are rumors about me going around the city, and it would mean so much to me if I didn't have to come here and see all those women whispering about me."

And when she finishes her plea, His response to her is simple and direct: "Go and get your husband" (John 4:16). The moment He says this, He disturbs her piece. He isn't being nosy or prying into her life. He isn't trying to embarrass her or shame her. He is disturbing the piece of her that is unstable. He is disturbing her instability. When she responds, "I don't have a husband," Jesus says, "You're right. You don't have a husband—for you have had five husbands, and you aren't even married to the man you're living with now" (John 4:17–18). That's pretty unstable!

They continue their conversation, and Jesus tells her how she can experience eternal and abundant life. Jesus doesn't make excuses for her behavior, nor does He blame her. He could have said, "You have a problem. Listen, you've had five husbands, and you're on your sixth. They are obviously not the issue." But He doesn't do that. Instead, Jesus kindly and lovingly addresses her instability. This woman's life is so upset that she runs back to the village and evangelizes to *everyone* about this Man who is so completely different from the six other men she has encountered. She tells them how a place in her life that has been perpetually unstable became stable because someone was bold enough to disturb her piece.

The place He picks is Samaria, the person He picks is the woman at the well, and the piece of her life He disturbs is her instability.

THE MOTHER-IN-LAW

In Matthew 8, we once again find Jesus on the road. This time He's going to Peter's house. "When Jesus arrived at Peter's house, Peter's mother-in-law was sick in bed with a high fever. But when Jesus touched her hand, the fever left her. Then she got up and prepared a meal for him" (vv. 14–15).

This is what I love about Jesus. He is just a regular Jewish guy who walks over to Peter's house, hears that his mother-in-law is sick, and decides to heal her. Peter didn't call Jesus over to his house and ask Him to heal his mother-in-law. Jesus chose to go to Peter's house, and He decided to disturb her piece. I think it may have gone down like this:

Jesus walks into the house and asks, "Hey! How's everybody doing?"

"Well, Peter's mother-in-law is in bed in the other room. She's sick with a high fever."

"Oh, she is?"

Jesus goes into the other room, takes her by the hand, and *immediately* the fever leaves her. Peter's mother-in-law is *completely* healed. She feels so good that she gets up out of bed and cooks everyone a meal.

We have opportunities nearly every day to disturb someone's piece. Maybe someone you know is sick or having a hard time. God might ask you to pray for them. Don't be a coward! Sometimes when God asks us to pray for someone, we let our insecurities get the best of us, and ridiculous thoughts and excuses like these run through our minds:

- *Uh, what if they don't want prayer? I don't want to get in a fight about it.*
- *I only can do it on my lunch break. What if there's not enough time?*
- *I have a headache. Maybe I should wait until I feel better.*

Don't overthink it. *Just pray for them.* And if you ask them if you can pray for them and they don't want you to, *pray for them anyway.* It's prayer—they don't have to hear it! You can pray for them when you're alone. They don't have to be right there with you.

So many people think you have to lay your hands on people when they're sick and pray dramatic prayers. "Jeeeeeesusssss!! Jesus! Jesus! Jesus! We come to you today, and we bind this horrible aching pain in her head, in Jesus' mighty, powerful name. Amen!" Don't be dramatic. *Just pray* for the person. "Lord, would you make her headache go away? Amen." Boom. Guess what? Heaven is not filled with people who are grading the word count on your prayers. God is not going to say to you, "Hey, John, there's a 50-word minimum word count for prayers, so you better keep praying! Oh, and you only said five "Father Gods," and I need to hear at least 20 of them before I'll heal her."

Listen, we need to stop the "Father God Prayers." When I hear Father God prayers, I forget what you were praying for because I'm now counting how many times you've said, "Father God." Instead of joining with you in prayer, what's really going through my mind is, *You're at 22 "Father Gods." Stop that and bless this food. It's cold now.*

I'm sure you know some "Father God" people. Their prayers sound like this: "Father God, in the name of Jesus, Father God, I come to you right now, Father God, because you know, Father God, you created us, Father God, because Father God, because Father God ... in Jesus' name, Father God, Father God, Amen." You know exactly what (and who) I'm talking about. Why do people do this? You would not go to McDonald's and stand in front of Robert, who is taking your order, and say, "Robert, oh Robert. Robert, can I have a Big Mac, Robert? Oooooohhhhh Robert. Robert, can I have a Big Mac? Oh, and Robert, I also need a large order of fries, Robert, because Robert, oh Robert,

Robert, Robert, I love French fries. Oh Robert, do you have the orange drink? Oooooooh Robert, Roooobert, Robert, Robert. Can I have two pies? Robert, Robert, Robert, Robert." Don't you see how ridiculous this is? Just pray! If you don't get this, you're going to upset the world in a different way.

When Jesus went to pray for Peter's mother-in-law, He didn't call down the heavens. He didn't say a "Father God" prayer. He simply touched her hand, and she was healed. That's all Jesus wants from us. He wants us to be obedient and to pray for people when He leads us, and He'll do the rest. We don't have to worry about how long we pray or how it sounds; we just need to be willing to disturb their piece.

The place He picks is Peter's house, the person He picks is his mother-in-law, and the piece of her life He disturbs is her sickness.

THE TAX COLLECTOR

In Luke 19, we find Jesus entering Jericho. As He's making His way through the town, He looks up and sees a short man in a tree. It's not just any short man. It's Zacchaeus, the chief tax collector and a man most people considered a crook. Jesus tells him to come down and invites Himself over to his house for dinner. "Zacchaeus quickly climbed down and took Jesus to his house in great excitement and joy. But the people were displeased. 'He has gone to be a guest of a notorious sinner,' they grumbled" (Luke 19:6–7).

The religious people are mad because Jesus is hanging out with a sinner. I love how much He doesn't care about what they think. Jesus already knew this man's reputation, but He decided to show up anyway. Just as He did in every single one of our lives. He knew our reputations, and He still said, "I know everything you've been through and everything you've done, and I still want to move in here with you." It's beautiful!

So Jesus goes to Zacchaeus's house and has dinner with him.

> Zacchaeus stood before the Lord and said, "'I will give half of my wealth to the poor, Lord, and if I had cheated people on their taxes, I will give them back four times as much!" Jesus responded, "Salvation has come to this home today, for this man has shown himself to be a true son of Abraham. For the Son of Man came to seek and save those who are lost" (Luke 19:8–10).

As chief tax collector, Zacchaeus had made a lot of money by overtaxing people. He became a very rich and wealthy man who had a lot of influence. He found his security and his identity in his wealth, but it was only covering a hole of rejection. You might be wondering, *Hey Tim, how did you conclude he dealt with rejection?* Truthfully, I don't know many short men who would climb up a tree just to get a peek of Jesus walking down the street. And then Jesus disturbed his piece—He noticed him! And when Jesus noticed him, he was so excited that he threw a dinner party for Him at his house! Zacchaeus had never been affirmed. And when he climbed that tree and Jesus said, "Hey, Zacchaeus! Come down! I want to come to your house today!" Zacchaeus must have thought, *What? Not because I'm rich? Not because of my influence in the community? But because **You saw me** in a tree?*

There are a lot of people in this world who are rich by the world's standards, but their identities are in their success. When your identity is found in your success, you're really covering up something on the inside of you that feels rejected. You turn to your vocation or your bank account or your degrees on the wall to affirm you, but those things will *never* affirm you like the One who created you. God not only affirms you, but He also fills you with His joy and peace (Romans 15:13).

> **When your identity is found in your success, you're really covering up something on the inside of you that feels rejected.**

Jesus decided to disturb the piece of rejection that was in Zacchaeus's heart. And here's how Zacchaeus responded: "Hey Jesus, I'll give half of my wealth to the poor." But he doesn't stop there. He goes on to say, and I love this, "And *if* I've robbed anybody ..." This is hilarious! Everybody, including Jesus, knew Zacchaeus didn't get rich because he did everything right. But if you understand Jewish context, then you know when he says, "I'll give them back four times as much!" that he was actually going *over and above* what Jewish law in the Pentateuch required for someone to pay restitution if they've been unfair with people. In reality, here's what he was saying: "I know I robbed people, and I want to make it right, so I'll go *above and beyond* what I'm required to give them back." And here's the moment you know Jesus is healing that piece of rejection on the inside of him. He looked at Zacchaeus and said, "You're a true son of Abraham. Not just because we could trace your bloodline back to him. Not because you're related to Abraham. But because you're acting like him. Acting like him shows you've placed your faith in Me."

The place He picks is Jericho, the person He picks is Zacchaeus, and the piece of his life He disturbs is his rejection.

EVERYONE

When they came to a place called The Skull, they nailed him to a cross. And the criminals were also crucified—one on his right and one on his left (Luke 23:33).
The place is the cross.

Jesus said, "Father forgive them, for they don't know what they are doing" (Luke 23:34).
The person is us.

Then Jesus shouted, "Father, I entrust my spirit into your hands!" And with those words He breathed his last (Luke 23:46).
The piece is sin.

What Jesus did for the woman at the well was absolutely amazing. He disturbed her piece of instability and gave her abundant life. She was no longer focused on *a man*; she was now focused on *the Man*.

What He did at Peter's house for his mother-in-law was nice. He's a nice guy, and He healed her sickness. He disturbed her piece of sickness and got her back on her feet, and things were good.

When He noticed a man in a tree and decided to go to his house to eat dinner—knowing his reputation and what people would say about Him in the process—that's just a guy who's so secure in His relationship with God that He doesn't care what people think. Yet Zacchaeus finds his whole world upset and turned upside down by a Jewish man who was just nice enough to have dinner with him and not think about His own reputation. He disturbed the piece of rejection Zacchaeus had been living with and gave him love and acceptance in return.

But this last one.

That He would go to Samaria, a place where no other Jews would go, for just one woman is amazing! That He would go to Peter's house just to heal his mother-in-law is nice. That He would go to Zacchaeus' house, a place no other Rabbi would go to a because he was such a disreputable man, is incredible! But let's just blow the lid off this thing right now.

That God would come to earth for us. *For you*. That the God of Heaven would wrap Himself in flesh and come here and dwell among us and then choose a place like the cross to display His love for us is almost too much to comprehend.

It would have been nice if He had just come into your house like He did with Zacchaeus. If Jesus would have spent the rest of all of human history just showing up at people's houses, that would have been nice. But for Him to show up to a cross and pick that place to display His love for all of us is something exponentially different.

If Jesus were to have been interviewed by a reporter before He died for us, I imagine the conversation may have sounded something like this:

Reporter: "Okay, You get to pick the place, Jesus. If You could give everyone a chance to understand Your love for us, what place would You pick?"

Jesus: "The cross."

Reporter: "Who would You die for? Because You know, there's a covenant with the Jewish people and that's who You've been called to, so if You're going to pick the cross and die a horrible death, a criminal's death, who are You going to do it for?"

Jesus: "Everybody."

Reporter: "And what piece would You like to disturb in that process, Jesus?"

Jesus: "Sin."

Reporter: "We saw what You did with instability. We saw what You did with sickness. And we saw what You did with rejection."

Jesus: "Yeah, yeah, yeah ... but that's all a result of sin. I don't want to go down a list of sins and check off each one individually. Let Me deal with *all sin*, so I can wipe it out for everybody. Then we'll have a huge family reunion with my Dad."

That Jesus would disturb the one piece that separates us from a relationship with God the Father on the cross, *intentionally for all of us*, is the most upsetting thing that has ever happened in all of human history. So much in fact that time has been split from before His death and after His death. The practice of BC and AD must have come from someone who understood there are a lot of people who lived and died, but Jesus's death and resurrection is the best thing that's ever happened!

> **"** That Jesus would disturb the one piece that separates us from a relationship with God the Father on the cross, *intentionally for all of us,* is the most upsetting thing that has ever happened in all of human history.

IT'S OUR TURN

Now it's our turn. We don't forgive people of their sins; Jesus has already done that. But we can disturb the piece that's blocking them from seeing the love of God in their lives. We are commissioned to go out and do it. It's not hard. It can actually be a lot of fun. And it starts with you intentionally picking the place.

I pick restaurants. I just pick two or three restaurants where I like to eat, and I decide to disturb people's piece. And you know how I start? I start with hugs. I hug everybody. I hug the hostess who is greeting people at the front of the restaurant. I hug the person who walks me to the table. I hug the waitress. *I hug everybody.* I go in there, hug everybody, eat, and leave a really good tip (*without* leaving a business card or an invitation to church). Then, when I come back, they say, "Hello! We're so glad you're here!" They remember me. Even if they just remember I'm the guy who hugs them, I've already started disturbing their piece.

If you start doing this, you'll begin to notice the waitstaff will fight over who gets to wait on you.

"He's here! I got him!"

"No, I got him!"

It's a full-on fight!

Sometimes I disturb people's piece the first time I meet them. Other times, it's the ninth time. There may be an opportunity where the Holy Spirit just gives me a sense of what's going on in their lives. He points out some fear, some intimidation, some rejection, some instability, and then He says, "I want you to disturb *that*!"

It doesn't matter whether you're introverted or extroverted. It's all the same. You simply ask the Holy Spirit to give you the boldness to go tinker with that piece a little bit.

I remember a time I was at The Cheesecake Factory, and a young lady was my server. I kept hearing the Holy Spirit say to me, "She's beautiful, she's beautiful, she's beautiful." Because I'm married, I wanted to be sure it was the Holy Spirit I was hearing. I didn't want to tell this young lady she's beautiful and give her the wrong impression. But He kept saying it over and over and over again until finally I said, "Okay, I'll tell her!"

I was there with one of my friends, so I turned to him and said, "Hey, I want to run this by you. I feel the Lord leading me to tell this young lady she's beautiful, but I don't want you to think I'm hitting on her. And if you say I shouldn't, then I won't."

He immediately said, "Go ahead and tell her."

So when she came back to our table, I said, "I just want to tell you that you're beautiful." She had a shocked look on her face, her eyes welled up with tears, and she left without saying anything. And she didn't come back for 10 minutes! My first thought was the manager was going to come over and chew me out because he thought I was hitting on one of his employees. But after 10 minutes, she came back to our table and said, "I was adopted as a baby, and for my whole life I've *never* felt like I was beautiful. And when you said that to me, it hit something deep down inside of me. I don't even know what to do with it."

I didn't turn this moment into a counseling session. I didn't start a prayer meeting in the middle of the restaurant. I simply said, "Well, I just felt like God told me to tell you that." Booya! I'm out. I'm not there to close the deal and rehabilitate her life. I'm just there to disturb the piece and let God do the rest.

God will give you opportunities like this, and He will give them to you according to your personality. You don't have to be a "hugger" like me. You don't have to go out and look for them. The Holy Spirit will let it happen, and He'll direct you to the place, the person, and the piece. You just have to have an open heart and be willing to be obedient as He leads you.

As upsetters, we all need to answer the question, "How do I disturb the piece?" First you have to pick the place. Where are you going to disturb them? Then you pick the person (or persons). Whom are you going to disturb? And lastly you pick the piece. What piece of their life are you going to upset?

Think about all these places Jesus went. It all started at a well. The woman shows up, and He says, "Give me some water." A conversation breaks out, and He disturbs her piece. He goes to Peter's house, and his wife's mom is sick. He decides to go to her room, pray for her, and she gets well. He walks down the road, sees Zacchaeus in a tree, and says, "Hey, Zacchaeus! Can I come to your home for dinner?" And Zacchaeus says, "Yes, let's go!" It's organic. It's natural. It's Spirit-led.

If you're at the gas station, and the Lord says something to you about someone there, go disturb their piece and then jump into your car and drive off. You don't have to turn it into a revival! I am simply encouraging you and exhorting you in a real way to go disturb the piece.

We need to be upsetters who will pick places and people and address the pieces in their lives they think are in harmony but really aren't. You probably already know some people who need to have their piece disturbed. You may have a co-worker, a family member, or a friend and you know there's a little piece in their life, that if it was disturbed, it would probably move stuff out of the way so they could see Jesus for who He really is.

Will you go out and disturb the piece? Because if we all do it, we'll be doing what God put us on earth to do, and it's how we're going to upset the world.

CHAPTER 9
UPSETTERS GET USED TO UPSETTING PEOPLE

*Lord, help me upset people every day
and everywhere I go. Amen.*

I stepped off the airplane and rushed out to the curb to catch my Uber. I had just enough time to get to my cousin's barbershop for a haircut before that night's church service. When I got into the car, the driver looked at me and said, "You're the best rider I've *ever* had in my car."

I had literally just sat down in his car and technically hadn't "ridden" anywhere, so I know the look on my face must have been one of complete confusion. I said, "I'm sorry, *what?*"

"You're the best rider I've ever had," he said. "I just sense something about you. I knew when you got in the car that you're a good man."

"Really?! How?"

"Because when I sent you a text message asking what terminal you're in, you replied 'Hi Bilal.' As long as I've been an Uber driver, no one has ever texted me and said 'Hi' and called me by my name. They usually just give me the terminal number, A28 or C21. And then when I arrive to pick them up, they get in the car and don't say two words to me. But you weren't like all the others. As soon as you wrote 'Hi Bilal,' I *knew* you were different."

I didn't do anything more than say hello and use his name, but I upset Bilal's world so much that it gave me an opportunity to talk with him. I found out he was from Lebanon and was driving for Uber to make extra money to provide for his family. He also asked a lot about me, so I shared about Embassy City and told him a little about myself and my family.

When we got to the barbershop, he said, "Hey, there's just something different about you, so here's what I want to do. I want to give charity rides on the weekends I'm free. If you know of anyone who needs a ride to church, I want you to call me, and I'll pick them up and bring them to church. No charge. I just want to do this."

All because I wrote "Hi Bilal." in a text message.

Did you notice I didn't have to ask Bilal from Lebanon whom he worshipped? I didn't have to ask him if he believed in God. I didn't say, "Let's figure that out first, and then I'll tell you about Jesus." I was just nice. I was kind. I was respectful. And it upset him. If we'll be this way in our interactions with people, they'll see Jesus in us, and this will upset them. **Remember, if we do good, the Holy Spirit will bring people to Jesus.**

SOME PEOPLE DON'T WANT TO BE UPSET

In order to upset the world, we have to get used to upsetting people. A natural byproduct of being an upsetter is upsetting people wherever we go. The more we become like Jesus, the more being an upsetter becomes part of our nature. It was in Jesus' nature to be an upsetter wherever He went. If we're Christ followers, we're naturally going to be upsetting people. Even people who don't want to be upset.

" The more we become like Jesus, the more being an upsetter becomes part of our nature.

This isn't anything new. Jesus also had to get used to upsetting people, even those who didn't want to be upset. We see one of these instances in Matthew 8:28–34 when He heals two demon-possessed men.

Jesus was walking through town when two men saw Him. These weren't just two normal guys; these men were possessed by demons and unusually violent. They were tormenting everyone who walked through this part of town, which made it very unsafe.

When the men saw Jesus, they looked at Him and said, "Ha! You're here early! We already know where we're going for eternity, and we know the clock's ticking, *but* that time has not come yet. Your blood hasn't been shed, and You haven't died. So what are You doing here? Why are you early? Are You here to *torment* us?"

They knew who Jesus was and the authority He carried with Him. He didn't even have to say a word. The demons sensed He was going to cast them out, so before He could even speak, they begged him, "Can we *please* go into the herd of pigs?"

And Jesus finally spoke, saying, "Okay, you scared little babies, go!"

And immediately the demons came out of the men and went into the herd of pigs. All 2,000 of them. The pigs proceeded to run down the hill, plunge into the lake, and drown.

Now, remember, Jesus upsets *everybody*. Walking through town, He upset the demons so much that they begged him to go into some pigs, and then they drowned in a lake. Obviously, they didn't think that through. They just knew that their power was no match for Jesus' power and authority. But Jesus not only upset them; He also upset an *entire town*!

After the herd of pigs drowned, the entire town came out to meet Jesus, but it wasn't to thank Him for saving these two men. It wasn't to celebrate their healing. It was just the opposite. They begged Jesus to go away and leave them alone. If you think about it, this is mind-blowing. These two men had been terrorizing the people in this section of town for so long that people stopped going this direction. Then Jesus comes in, frees the men, and makes it a safe area. But when the herdsmen went back into the city and told everyone they were safe, the people responded, "Huh? What just happened?"

"You know those two men who have been terrorizing us all these years? They're healed! They're free! They're not crazy anymore, and they're not going to terrorize us. We're safe now! The demons are gone. Jesus did it. This Guy right here—He did it!"

And the entire town went out to meet Jesus, and said, "Hey, You need to go!" They begged and pleaded for Him to go away and leave them alone.

To me, this is more mind-blowing than Jesus healing the two men from demons. I mean, why did they want Jesus to go? He just proved that if He did it for these guys, He could do it for everybody in the city!

Are you ready for it? **Some people don't want you to upset their world**. They like it the way it is. They are so used to their lifestyle that even though they just saw the most amazing miracle, they want things to stay the same. Change can be uncomfortable and shocking. If it looks like it's going to be too much work for people if things change or if it gets too uncomfortable, they just might ask you to leave.

If you're going to upset the world, you have to get used to upsetting people—even people who don't want to be upset. The truth is, it doesn't matter if they don't receive it. If you prayed for them and it's completely evident that God is moving in the situation, but they don't want to be upset, you're going to have to be okay with it. This takes some time getting used to and is something I've had to deal with in my own life, even when I know it's something the Lord told me to do.

Sometimes the Holy Spirit prompts me to do things that are sure to upset people, and I don't always know how they're going to respond. One of the things I hear a lot is to pay for the groceries of the person in line behind me. I've done this so many times I'm now sleek at it. I move down to where my bags are waiting for me, and whether I have two items or ten, I start acting like I'm double-checking my bags until I hear the cashier say, "Your total is ..." Then as they move to the right, I move to the left, stick my card in the slot, and bam! I've paid for their groceries! They almost always ask, "Why did you do that?" And my answer is almost always, "I just want to bless you" or sometimes I say "For no reason at all. Are you upset?!"

A few years ago, when I was in California, I stopped by a grocery store in a very well-to-do neighborhood to pick up a few items. I was at the cash register paying for my groceries when I noticed a lady in line behind me. Immediately, I felt that familiar prompting from the Lord, and I knew He was telling me to pay for her groceries. I finished checking out, and as the cashier scanned her groceries, I just stood there at the end of the conveyor belt fumbling with my bags and acting like I was having trouble picking them up. I was timing it out so I could make my move.

Beep ... beep ... beep. Finally, the last can of corn goes across the belt, and with one final beep, she was done. The cashier said, "It's going to be $43.97," and it's then I knew it was time to make my move. Before she knew what was happening, I stepped in front of her and swiped my credit card.

To say the lady was shocked is an understatement. "What did you just do?!" she snapped at me.

"I just wanted to bless you today."

"I don't need to be blessed. *Why* did you just do that?" she demanded.

"Really, I just wanted to be a blessing to you today," I said, still a bit confused how a person could be so offended by someone paying for their groceries.

"Well, I don't need your blessing. Next time, do it for somebody who really needs it, because I don't need it."

I had a million thoughts running through my mind, but I finally said. "Are we really going to argue right now about me paying for your groceries? I *know* you don't need it. I just wanted to do it. I *wanted* to bless you!"

"Well, whatever. Thank you," she said tersely. And that's how our conversation ended.

I grabbed my bags and walked away, feeling as if I had just wasted my time and my money. I knew from experience that people who are well off are often the hardest people to bless. But this was ridiculous! I was about to have a "come to Jesus" conversation with the Man Himself, because I felt like the Holy Spirit led me to do that, and it's not the reaction I typically get from people.

As soon as I got outside, I looked up and said, "Jesus, I didn't like the way that went down. Why did You lead me to bless her? From now on, I only want to bless people who like being blessed. That was rough!"

And it was almost like He crept to the edge of His seat next to His Dad, leaned over, and said, "Now you know how I feel. I didn't go to the cross because I knew you would come to Me. I went to the cross that you might."

SOME PEOPLE DO WANT TO BE UPSET

There is good news! There are people who really do want to be upset. They want healing and freedom. They want their world to change. Remember the story in the last chapter about Jesus and the Samaritan woman (John 4:1–30)? Jesus told her to go and get her husband. She told him she didn't have a husband, and He said she was right. She had had five husbands, and she wasn't married to the man she was currently living with. He told her things about herself that only He could know, and it completely upset her.

She wasn't angry. On the contrary, she was so happy and excited about what had just happened that she dropped her water bucket and ran back to the village and told everyone she could find what had happened. She had found healing and hope. The people came streaming from the village to see Jesus. They wanted their lives changed in the same way hers was. Whatever she had found, they wanted it too. They weren't angry or afraid either. They were happy and came to celebrate what had taken place.

In one scenario, Jesus walks through a town, He sees two men who have demons, they recognize him, and He casts them out. They run and tell everyone in the village, and the people are like, "Nope, we're not interested in that." So Jesus leaves. In another, He meets a woman who had a lot of relationships and can't figure out why. He talks to her, she drops her water bucket, goes back to the village and tells her story of hope and healing to everyone, and the whole city comes to find Jesus. *They wanted to be upset.* They knew her and the kind of person she was before she had her life upset, and they knew if Jesus could do that for her, He could it for them too.

It's so much fun to upset people who want to be upset. It's something my best friend, Korey, and I love to do more than anything. Back when we were both single, we did *everything* together. I didn't have a car, so he had to take me everywhere. He would pick me up at my apartment and take me to church or to restaurants or wherever. (He was my Uber before there was Uber!) One of the things we have in common is we're both givers. We *love* to bless people.

One time, we went to lunch at a local restaurant to eat dinner and hang out. At the end of the meal, we got the check and were talking about how much we should tip. Here we are, two young, single guys living on a budget but trying to be generous, since we love to bless people. Korey asks me what I'm going to leave for a tip. I hadn't decided yet, so I asked what he was going to leave.

"I'm going to give her $20.00."

"What?! You're going to give her $20? Our meal didn't even cost $20!"

"Yeah, well, it's what I'm going to do," he shot back.

"I'm going to give her $20 too!" I mean, I couldn't let him out-bless me.

So we paid our bill, and each left her a $20 tip—$40 total. But instead of leaving, we stayed at the table and kept talking. We've gotten better about this through the years, but at that time we were both novices at blessing the waitstaff. Now we don't actually like to be around when the waiter or waitress gets the tip. We like to be gone. Like Batman, we just disappear.

It wasn't long before our waitress came back to our table. With tears in her eyes, she explained how this was only her second day on the job and the tips we left her were the biggest tips she'd ever received working at any restaurant. She thanked us profusely and asked, "Who are you guys?"

We told her we just wanted to bless her and that we loved her and were praying for her. She couldn't believe we didn't want anything from her or that there wasn't some catch. We weren't hitting on her. We didn't want to date her. We weren't looking for a discount the next time we came to eat there. The world doesn't understand upsetters. The world is so cynical that they want to know, "What's the catch? Why are you doing something nice for me? There must be more to this!" The truth is, we simply wanted to bless her. We wanted to show her how valuable her service was to us, and we wanted her to know her value and worth.

You see, we upset her in the best way possible way. She was completely overturned. The reality is you upset some people, and they receive it. You upset other people, and they don't receive it. It's not our assignment to size up people and figure who's going to receive it and who's not. It's simply our assignment to upset.

> **❝** It's not our assignment to size up people and figure who's going to receive it and who's not. It's simply our assignment to upset.

UPSETTERS GET OTHERS TO UPSET PEOPLE

Korey and I also have a love for fashion in common. I have always liked to dress sharp. I enjoy looking put together and wearing clothes that are in style, and I always like a nice tailored suit. Before I was married, I didn't have a lot of clothes, and the ones I did have didn't look so nice. Korey, on the other hand, has always been a very nice dresser and has always owned very stylish clothes. One time, I went into his apartment, and as I was admiring his clothes, I saw a shirt hanging up that I really wanted to wear. So I asked him, "Can I wear this shirt?"

Without hesitating, he said, "No, never! You can't. Why would I ever let you wear my clothes?!"

"Because I'm your best friend, and I look very tacky."

"That's never going to happen! I love you, but you're not wearing my clothes."

And he never did let me wear his clothes. I know you probably thought I was about to tell you there was a time he let me, but no, it didn't happen! But now that I'm married and have a good job, I can afford to have some decent clothes. And one of my very favorite places to shop is Zar. This upscale boutique is tucked away in Southlake Town Square, just outside of Dallas. The store is owned by Roy, a wonderfully nice Pakistani man who is a Muslim.

Whenever I'm on that side of town, I almost always stop by, even if I don't plan to buy anything. A couple of years ago, I stopped in to see what new things had come in that week. Since it's a semi-couture clothier, they only get a few sizes of each piece. So if you see something you like, you need to buy it, or else it may not be there the next time you come in. Once it's gone, it's gone.

As I was walking around the store, I overheard a young man named Chris talking with one of Roy's salesmen, John. He was fitting him for a suit, and Chris began telling him all about his new job. Once he had the suit on, I looked over and saw it. He looked great! After talking with John for a few more minutes, he went back into the dressing room and changed out of his suit. As he was changing, I heard John say, "The suit looks great on you! Are you going to be able to get it today?"

Chris stepped out of the dressing room with the new suit draped over his arm, walked over to John, put his arm out and said, "Actually, no. I love the suit, but like I was telling you, I just started a new job. Give me a few weeks to earn some money, and then I'll come back and buy it."

As I stood there listening to their conversation, I thought, *Wow! For a young man who's just starting a career to have that level of discipline is pretty amazing. It's a really nice suit, and it looks great on him! Surely it fits in the corporate structure where he's working now.*

And then it happened. That all too familiar Holy Spirit prompting. I heard Him say, "Buy that young man the suit."

My first thought was, *Are You sure? Because I came to buy a shirt for myself!*

He said it again, "I want you to buy the suit for him."

I called John and Roy over and told them I wanted to pay for his suit, but I didn't want them to tell Chris who paid for it. They were shocked, but they agreed.

As John goes over to the register to ring up the suit, I grab a shirt off the rack, go into the dressing room, and listen. I hear John say to the young man, "We just want to bless you with the suit. It's yours."

He was stunned, "What? Are you sure?"

"Yes," he stammered. "We just want to bless you."

After Chris took his suit and left the store, I came out of the dressing room and paid for it.

Not long after this happened, Chris came back to Zar and badgered Roy and John about who paid for the suit until they finally gave in and shared my name with him. It wasn't long before he tracked me down and called me on my cell phone. "I just want to say thank you. Maybe I can take you out to lunch or something," he said. So we went to lunch and had a nice conversation, and that was that. Or so I thought.

Ten months later, I'm back shopping at Zar one Saturday afternoon when I hear someone behind me say, "That's the guy right there, Mom!" I turned around to see Chris standing there with his parents, who were in town visiting from Missouri.

"There's the dude who bought me the suit," he said again, this time with even more enthusiasm.

"Oh my goodness! We've been hearing about the suit story for the past year! What you did was the nicest thing ever!" his mom, Michelle, said.

We all hug, they thank me profusely, and then Michelle says, "We're all going to your church tomorrow!"

The next day, they showed up at Embassy City, and they loved it! They went back home a few days later and started listening to all of our church podcasts. They wanted to share it with others, so they decided to host a small group in their neighborhood. Every week, a group gathered at their house to listen and discuss that week's podcast.

About 18 months later, the Lord started speaking to Michelle about starting a ministry called Rise & Go to help disenfranchised kids in her community. She started by creating a community garden so people in the area could have fresh fruits and vegetables. Then she put on her first big event in September 2018, and she invited me to come and share a message with the kids. She also invited two other Christian guys, one from the MMA who shared with the kids and a BMX biker who did tricks. It was the coolest event! And she did it all so the kids could have an opportunity to hear the gospel. She wanted to upset them in the same way she'd been upset.

You see, upset people get others to upset people. When you've had your life overturned, it's impossible to act like nothing happened. Even the guys at Zar were upset. While they haven't become Christians yet, the seed has been deeply planted. (We'll talk more about planting and harvesting in the next chapter.) When I obeyed the Holy Spirit and gave Chris the suit, God not only did something in my heart, but He also started doing something in their hearts. They now bless other people who come into the store. They tell everyone the "suit story," they give away shirts, and they have been known to give deep discounts and charge people less for the clothes than their cost. Every time I come in, they ask me to pray for them, and they tell people to go to church at Embassy City. Why are they doing this? Because upsetters get others to upset people.

" Upsetters get others to upset people.

One day you might type "Hi Bilal" or buy a lady's groceries or leave your waitress a large tip or buy a young man a suit and upset their world so much that they start upsetting others.

CHAPTER 10
UPSETTERS UPSET THE WORLD

Holy Spirit, go with me as I follow Your command
to upset the world. Amen.

I ministered at a church in St. Louis one weekend, and they gave me a gift basket filled with all kinds of goodies, including a $100 gift card. When I was packing to go home, I threw the card in my duffle bag. Later that day, as I was going through security at the airport, I noticed a guy in a military uniform. Instantly, the Holy Spirit spoke and told me to give him the gift card. By that time, the guy was putting his boots back on, so not wanting to waste any time, I started rummaging through my bag to find the card before he could walk away. By the time I found it, however, he had already left for his gate.

Our plane was scheduled to depart from Gate C6, but I saw him walk in the opposite direction. Now I had a decision to make. I could obey what the Holy Spirit was telling me to do, or I could choose to go the opposite direction to my gate and ensure I wouldn't miss my flight. Two things crossed my mind. One, I wanted to obey what the Lord was telling me to do. And two, I wanted to upset this guy's world. So, without running through the airport and making a scene, I decided to walk as quickly as possible and follow him to his gate. (Although as he kept walking, I'll admit I kept thinking, *Get to your gate already!*) He finally got to his gate—C27!

He sat down, put his bag down beside his feet, and put his headphones on the chair beside him. I knew it was time to make my move. I walked up to where he was sitting, lifted up his headphones, put the gift card under them, and before he could even say a word, put his headphones back down. I shook his hand and said, "Thank you for your service." Then I walked away. He didn't have time to ask me what I was doing or who I was. He just looked up me and said, "Thank you" as I was leaving. I didn't wait around and spend time witnessing to him. I was just planting a seed.

UPSETTERS SOW SEEDS

If you've been a Christian for any amount of time, I'm sure you've heard a pastor or teacher talk about "reaping the harvest." This is an expression taken from Matthew 9:38 when Jesus said to His disciples, "The harvest is great, but the workers are few. So pray to the Lord who is in charge of the harvest; ask him to send more workers into his fields." I've noticed, more so in recent years, that there's a romanticism with the harvest and winning souls, but seedtime and irrigation have almost been forgotten.

This has become even more amplified to me in recent months as I've watched Juliette start a garden in our backyard. She put in fresh soil, planted the seeds, watered the plants as they grew, pulled weeds, and made sure the garden got plenty of sunlight. She let nothing go to waste, not even the weeds. She pulled them up, let them dry until they turned brown, and then put them in the compost machine. She then took the compost and put it back into the dirt, giving the soil nutrients that helped the plants grow. She meticulously tended to it daily until it was time to gather the harvest. She loves the whole process of growing her own food and makes sure each step is completed with care.

If Juliette were only in love with the harvest, then she'd just go to our local supermarket, because that's where the harvest is. If she wanted organic tomatoes and couldn't wait, she'd go buy them. She would let someone else do all the work for her and would enjoy the fruits of their labor.

This is like many of the Christians I know today. They don't want to do the work it takes to reap a harvest, but they want to enjoy the fruits of someone else's labor. Truth be told, we've become lazy. We're trying to harvest what someone else put in the work to do. Someone else planted. Someone else irrigated the land. Someone else picked it off the vine. Someone else did all the work.

The harvest belongs to God, and He's the one who gets credit for it. Paul said,

> Each of us did the work the Lord gave us. I planted the seed in your hearts, and Apollos watered it, but it was God who made it grow. It's not important who does the planting, or who does the watering. What's important is that God makes the seed grow (1 Corinthians 3:6–7).

God is the one who gets the credit for the increase. The truth is if you're not planting the seeds, all you're doing is plucking the fruit off the tree.

> **❝ The truth is if you're not planting the seeds, all you're doing is plucking the fruit off the tree.**

There's a mistake many of us tend to make when we think about evangelism. We think only about the harvest—that salvation moment—when there's actually an entire agricultural process involved. We forget about sowing (sharing the gospel) and watering (treating someone with kindness and love and praying for them) because these steps don't seem as exciting as harvesting. However, God has given all of us the gifts of sowing and watering as well as harvesting. In fact, it's so important that Jesus instructed us to sow the seed of the gospel *everywhere* we go.

> Listen! A farmer went out to plant some seeds. As he scattered them across his field, some seeds fell on a footpath, and the birds came and ate them. Other seeds fell on shallow soil with underlying rock. The seeds sprouted

quickly because the soil was shallow. But the plants soon wilted under the hot sun, and since they didn't have deep roots, they died. Other seeds fell among thorns that grew up and choked out the tender plants. Still other seeds fell on fertile soil, and they produced a crop that was thirty, sixty, and even a hundred times as much as had been planted! (Matthew 13:3–8).

If we take His parable literally, it's *really terrible* farming advice, because the sower doesn't care whether the ground is thorny or stony; he just throws the seeds everywhere! So many of us are worried about making the seed stick or explaining our faith in a way that people can *get* it, but those are the jobs of the Holy Spirit. Our job is simply to sow the seed.

For years, I've gotten pedicures on a regular basis at the Four Seasons Spa. (I know, I know. I'm bougie, and I'm okay with that.) Then, not too long ago, I found a girl who owns a small nail spa that's closer to my office. Her place is the size of a crackerjack box. There are only two rooms, and the whole place is void of all the fancy equipment at the Four Seasons, but she does a better job than any of those other girls. And she charges a third of the price.

I've only been to her place a few times, but each time we've engaged in conversation the whole time I was there. We're both from California, and that's about where our similarities stop. She hasn't been going to church since she moved to Texas because she found the churches to be full of hypocrites. I've heard her say more than once, "People don't really live like that." Instead of pushing her to visit our church, I spend my appointments talking with her and sharing about how my life's been upset by Jesus. I just keep sowing seeds.

At the end of my last appointment, she said, "I'm going to come to your church." While I was happy to hear her say that, I'm not going to be standing at the church door looking for her. I don't need to make sure she gets to church so she can hear a soul-stirring message. I know she doesn't have to be in church for Jesus to upset her life. Honestly, there's more going on during our conversations while she's doing my feet than anything she might get out of going to church.

If we're going to upset the world, we have to be able to bring the gospel message to where people are. We can't keep waiting for evangelism week at church to talk to people about Jesus. We can't wait for a great podcast to come out so we can tell our neighbors, "Oh, you need to listen to this podcast. It will change your life!" No, *you* can change their life right where they are with the message of Jesus Christ.

Each time I see my pedicure girl, I plant another seed and upset her just a little more. We talk, and I listen for the lie she's believing and just chip away at it. Sometimes I feel the Holy Spirit say, "Push back on 'that' a little bit." All this is happening while she's taking care of my toes. I have a captive audience. And I believe one day, the seeds I've been planting and the irrigation I've been doing will pay off in a *big* harvest.

UPSETTERS SHOW PEOPLE
HOW TO CHANGE THEIR CLOTHES

One of the most fascinating parables Jesus ever told is about the great feast in Matthew 22:1–14. He was talking to the religious leaders of His day, the ones who had moved away from the type of relationship God wanted to establish when He brought them out of Egypt so they could worship Him and have a one-on-one relationship with Him. But He's also talking to us.

In this parable, Jesus tells us about a king who decides to throw a wedding feast for his son and invites a lot of guests. However, none of the invited guests want to come. The king is furious! "I've been sent to you to call you into this wedding feast so we could all be together. I've sent the invitations out, but you don't want to come. And since you don't want to come, I'm going to invite some other people."

I love how this parable is set up. The king has invited specific guests, people he has a relationship with, to this feast. But since they refused to come, he's just going to invite *anybody!* He said, "Listen, go call everybody! Call anybody who wants to come. Not just good people. People who are nice and have good demeanors. Call some bad people too. Call some thugs. Call some gangsters. Call some hustlers. Call some white-collar criminals. Call some hackers. *Call everybody*!" And all of these people come in droves to this party. Why? Because there is going to be a feast!

And all of these people, unintended guests, show up to this party. And the king comes down to meet them, and he notices one of the guests doesn't have on the right clothes. I love the way he addresses him, even though he'd never met him and didn't have a covenant with him: "'Friend,' he asked, 'how is it that you are here without wedding clothes?'" (Matthew 22:12).

And the man says nothing.

It's interesting that he doesn't have a reply. I'm pretty fast on my feet, and I imagine I'd have something to say if the king asked me a question. But this man has nothing to say. It's astonishing!

The king is obviously not happy and responds by saying, "Bind his hands and feet and throw him into the outer darkness, where there will be weeping and gnashing of teeth" (Matthew 22:13).

If you're like me, you're probably wondering why the king is so harsh. The truth is the king's actions are justified. There was no king, or anyone for that matter, with that amount of wealth who would throw an invitation out to the public and assume people had the right clothes to wear. The king would purchase garments for everyone who was attending, and when they arrived at the feast, their garments would be provided for them at the door. As they walked in, the servants on either side of the door would say, "Thank you for accepting this invitation. Here are the garments for this party. Please go inside and change your clothes."

You see, the invitation is "come as you are," but the implication is "you can't stay as you are." The invitation is "all are welcome," but the invitation is also "you can't stay the same." The invitation is "I'll take you wherever you currently are. I don't care if you have a Bible in your hand, a blunt in your hand, or a bat in your hand ... *just come*. We'll work out the rest later."

So when the king comes down, and everyone has changed their clothes except this one man, it implies to me that he is filled with obstinance and rebellion. Truthfully, this man's "no reply" *is* a reply. He is essentially saying, "I saw the clothes you had there, and I didn't like them. They're really not my style."

But then the king doesn't just uninvite him; he says, "Throw him into outer darkness!" While Jesus is talking to the religious leaders when He tells this story, He's really communicating to *everyone* who would ever be invited to the table—Jews *and* Gentiles. For you see, the king in this story represents God. And I love that after God's intended demographic, the Jews, didn't want to accept His love, He didn't just go look for one other specific group of people. No, He opened it up to *everybody*— Jews *and* Gentiles! Romans 5:8 says, "But God showed his great love for us by sending Christ to die for us while we were still sinners." When He gives an invitation, He knows you're not in right standing with Him. He knows you're disconnected from Him. When He gives an invitation, He calls you right where you are. He's not waiting for you to clean up before you show up. All He's saying is you can come right now, with whatever you're struggling with, with whatever habits you have, whatever dysfunctionalities you have, whatever clothes you have on.

Come right now. It's a beautiful thing to receive an invitation to a party that you were originally not invited to and you get to show up just as you are.

> **"** He's not waiting for you to clean up
> before you show up.

He calls you like you are, but He doesn't have any expectation that you'll stay as you are. Romans 13:12–14 says:

> The night is almost gone; the day of salvation will soon be here. So remove your dark deeds like dirty clothes, and put on the shining armor of right living. Because we belong to the day, we must live decent lives for all to see. Don't participate in the darkness of wild parties and drunkenness, or in sexual promiscuity and immoral living, or in quarreling and jealousy. Instead, clothe yourself with the presence of the Lord Jesus Christ. And don't let yourself think about ways to indulge your evil desires.

See, He takes you just as you are, but He has no intention of allowing you to stay just as you are.

"Come as you are" is the evangelistic message of the gospel, but "you can't stay as you are" is the discipleship message of the gospel. We want everyone to come, but we don't want anybody to stay the same. There is something happening in 2019 Christianity that we want people in church so badly that we won't even tell them to change their clothes. We want people to be in community and in our churches, but we don't want to offend anyone. So we say, "Whatever you have on is fine. I don't care what it is; it's fine." And that's true ... **whatever you have on is fine enough for you to come to Jesus, but it won't be good enough for you to stay here.**

People have to choose whether or not they want to change their clothes. Romans 6:16 says, "Don't you realize that you become the slave of whatever you choose to obey? You can be a slave to sin, which leads to death, or you can choose to obey God, which leads to righteous living." God won't make someone change, and you can't either. It has to be their decision. God sent His Son to die on the cross that we *might* have life (1 John 4:9 paraphrase). That maybe, perhaps, if the person you've been planting seeds in could really see the extravagant gift Jesus displayed on the cross, then maybe, just maybe, they'd come into a relationship with Him, and perhaps one day, change their clothes. But *they* have to make a choice.

YOUR ASSIGNMENT

As believers, we've *all* been called to upset the world. We don't have to ask the Lord if it's something He's called us to do. There's no need to pray and fast about it. He's clearly said in His Word that we're to "go and make disciples" (Matthew 28:18). The Bible calls this "The Great Commission," but it could also be called "Go Upset the World." It's what Jesus told His followers, including you and me, to do.

Jesus came and told his disciples, "I have been given all authority in heaven and on earth. Therefore, go and make disciples of all the nations, baptizing them in the name of the Father and the Son and the Holy Spirit. Teach these new disciples to obey all the commands I have given you. And be sure of this: I am with you always, even to the end of the age" (Matthew 28:16–20).

Jesus is essentially saying, "Hey, you ... the one whose life has been upset ... I want to give you *all* the authority in heaven *and* on earth to go upset the world!" That's seriously a lot of power and authority. Jesus didn't give you just a little bit of authority. He gave you *all* authority. In heaven *and* earth. Think about that? You have more power than any Marvel or DC comic superhero. More than Superman, Spiderman, Batman, Iron Man, and Wonder Woman combined! All you have to do is take this authority and use it for good. And the way you do that is by upsetting people's worlds.

Look at this part of the passage again: "Teach these new disciples to obey all the commands I have given you" (Matthew 28:20). You know what that command is? To go upset the world. Here's what Jesus is saying, "The thing that you saw Me do for three and a half years before I went to the cross? That's what you'll be doing. And I want you to command others and teach others to do it as well. Teach these new disciples to obey all that I have given you and be sure of this, I am with you always, even to the end of the age." An upsetter is someone who's been upset and upsets others. Here's how Paul says it in 2 Timothy 2:2:

> You have heard me teach things that have been confirmed by many reliable witnesses. Now teach these truths to other trustworthy people who will be able to pass them on to others.

This is why I wrote this book. If there's one thing that has completely rocked my world in my walk with the Lord, it's the revelation that we've been called to upset the world. It makes so much sense to me. I've never seen anything plainer in the 20-plus years I've been saved and preaching the gospel of Jesus Christ. And the reason why it's so easy for me to talk about is because the Holy Spirit is the one who revealed it to me. He said, "I want you to teach this message to people. But here's the thing I want you to know, Tim. I've already been using you to upset the world. You've been doing this your whole life."

I'm not talking about doing sensationalistic things. I know people whom God has used to raise the dead. I've read documented miracles about people who didn't have a limb, and then their whole arm grew out into a hand. I wish I could tell you I had miraculous stories like this to share with you. I don't. It's never happened to me. But when the Holy Spirit said to me, "Do you know I've already been using you to upset the world?" I became undone. I had a fire in my belly that couldn't be quenched.

A lot of times we think that unless we're casting out demons or doing something sensationalistic that we're not being mightily used by God. However, that couldn't be farther from the truth. He uses us all in different ways. Sometimes the Holy Spirit will lead you to do something as simple as giving someone a gift card, or sometimes He'll lead you to do something more involved such as building a relationship with someone. What's important is that you hear and obey what He says, because the way we're going to upset the world is by obeying the leading of the Holy Spirit.

> **❝ The way we're going to upset the world is by obeying the leading of the Holy Spirit.**

I hope this book has equipped you with everything you need to upset the world and that you would be bold and, through the Holy Spirit, go out and upset others with the message, love, and hope of Jesus Christ. Don't let anything or anyone stop what God has called you to do. **Expressing your faith can change the world.**

I encourage you to take some time to pray about whom the Holy Spirit wants you to upset. Ask Him to put some people in your path this week, or even today, whom you can upset. Just like the sower in the parable, take a handful of seed and *chuck* it! And then ask the Holy Spirit, "What's my assignment? Am I sowing, watering, or harvesting?" As you steward your role in the agricultural process of evangelism, you might do a little of each. It's all a matter of listening to His voice and following where He leads. If you do this, you will upset the world!

EPILOGUE

Lord, when times get hard,
help me remember Your plans for my life. Amen.

As you start out on your journey to upset the world, I want to make sure you go out with the knowledge and understanding of how much God loves you and that He has great plans for your life. When the enemy comes against you—and he will—and tries to overthrow you, you can stand with your feet firmly planted on this Scripture:

> "For I know the plans I have for you," says the Lord. "They are plans for good and not for disaster, to give you a future and a hope" (Jeremiah 29:11).

There will be seasons in your life as an upsetter when it will be hard for you to embrace the things God has said about you, but I'm here to remind you that you *are* God's masterpiece. It's not my opinion; it's fact. Ephesians 2:10 says, "For we are God's masterpiece. He has created us anew in Christ Jesus, so we can do the good things he planned for us long ago." This can be kind of hard to wrap your mind around because you know yourself better than anyone. You know the good and the bad thoughts you have, and you know the good and the bad things you do. But the good news is that when you allowed Jesus to come into your life and turn it upside down, He made you new. He doesn't see your old, sinful nature. Second Corinthians 5:17 says, "Anyone who belongs to Christ has become a new person. The old life is gone; a new life has begun!"

God has a plan for all of us. He has a plan for surfers, librarians, IT nerds, gamers, CEOs, hunters, entrepreneurs, stay-at-home moms, students, and neurosurgeons. He has plans for *everybody*, even *you*! The plans God has for each of us are so profound. Remember, you don't have to be a preacher or an evangelist to be used by God. Jesus didn't die to upset the whole world so that everybody could be in the pulpit preaching. There are more people in the marketplace who need Jesus than I'll ever see sitting in a pew at church. His plans for each one of us are to be strategically used in the place of our expertise, the place of our passion to reach people for His name.

And that's really the reason we're all here: to upset the world with the message, love, and hope of Jesus Christ. If you get this, you *will* upset the world.

This book is dedicated to Embassy City Church and its ambassadors. Thank you for being committed to turning the world upside down.

ABOUT THE AUTHOR

Tim Ross is the lead pastor of the multi-ethnic, multi-generational Embassy City Church in Irving, Texas. He began preaching at the age of 20 and has already impacted the lives of hundreds of thousands of people. Tim speaks both nationally and internationally, strengthening believers with the Good News of Jesus Christ. His dynamic teaching style and uncanny ability to make people understand the gospel message is the reason why he has been such an asset to ministries across cultural and denominational lines. Tim and his wife, Juliette, have been happily married for over 20 years, and they are the proud parents of two sons, Nathan and Noah.

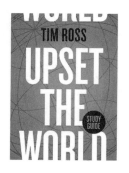

Also Available:

Upset the World Study Guide
978-1-951227-08-1

gatewaypublishing.com